BPEL Cookbook
Best Practices for SOA-based integration and composite applications development

Ten practical real-world case studies combining business process management and web services orchestration

Editors

Harish Gaur, Markus Zirn

Authors

*Stany Blanvalet, Jeremy Bolie, Michael Cardella, Sean Carey,
Praveen Chandran, Yves Coene, Kevin Geminiuc, Matjaž B. Jurič,
The Hoa Nguyen, Arun Poduval, Lawrence Pravin, Jerry Thomas, Doug Todd*

PUBLISHING

BIRMINGHAM - MUMBAI

BPEL Cookbook: Best Practices for SOA-based integration and composite applications development

First published: July 2006

Production Reference: 2140706

Published by Packt Publishing Ltd.
32 Lincoln Road
Olton
Birmingham, B27 6PA, UK.

ISBN 1-904811-33-7

www.packtpub.com

Cover Image by www.visionwt.com

Credits

About the Editors

Harish Gaur [harish.gaur@oracle.com] has more than 10 years of experience in the enterprise software industry. He is currently the Group Product Manager for Fusion Middleware at Oracle. In his current role, he works closely with strategic customers implementing Service-Oriented Architecture using Oracle SOA technology. Harish's expertise in Service-Oriented Architecture (SOA) draws from an extensive hands-on experience with Business Process Management (BPM) and Enterprise Application Integration (EAI).

Before Oracle, he worked as a Solution Specialist with Vitria Technology educating customers about the benefits of Business Process Management. Prior to that, he helped Fortune 500 companies architect scalable integration solutions using EAI tools like webMethods and CrossWorlds (now IBM). Harish holds an engineering degree in Computer Science and is an MBA from Haas School of Business, UC Berkeley. He lives in Fremont, CA with his wife Swati and son Agastya.

Markus Zirn [markus.zirn@oracle.com] is a Senior Director of Product Management for Oracle Fusion Middleware. In this role he heads the Strategic Customer Program, where he works with Oracle's leading and most innovative middleware customers. He has been part of the Enterprise Software industry for more than 10 years, including roles as Vice President of Product Marketing and part of the founding team of QUIQ and as a Management Consultant of Booz Allen & Hamilton's Silicon Valley High Tech Practice.

Markus' passion for Service-Oriented Architecture (SOA) and BPEL stems both from practical experience designing and optimizing business processes as part of process reengineering projects and from being part of the advent of "software as a service" before web services became mainstream. He holds a Masters of Electrical Engineering from the University of Karlsruhe and is an alumnus of the Tripartite program, a joint European degree from the University of Karlsruhe, Germany, the University of Southampton, UK, and ESIEE, France.

About the Authors

Stany Blanvalet [stany.blanvalet@jaisy.be] is a BPEL and J2EE consultant. Previously, working as a Java EE architect, Stany introduced and administered Belgacom's BPEL-based DSL provisioning application, a mission-critical BPEL production system. He is a contributor to the Jaisy-ORABPEL Interface project , an open-source JMX monitoring tool for Oracle BPEL Process Manager. Stany Blanvalet contributed Chapter 10.

Jeremy Bolie [jbolie@qualcomm.com] is a Senior IT Manager at QCT, managing the custom applications and Documentum development team. Jeremy has over 10 years of experience with Java and Oracle technologies, and has been involved with web services and Service-Oriented Architectures since the late 1990s. Jeremy Bolie and Michael Cardella worked together on Chapter 9.

Michael Cardella [c_mcarde@qualcomm.com] is a Staff Engineer at Qualcomm CDMA Technologies (QCT). Michael works in the custom applications development team, primarily on web-service- and business-process-related applications. Previously he served as Principal Architect for a leading web services security and management product.

Sean Carey [scarey@spscommerce.com] is a Software Architect at SPS Commerce, a leader in hosted EDI. Sean has over seven years of experience in mission-critical e-commerce implementations, and 15 years of industry experience in software design. Sean Carey gave us Chapter 7.

Praveen Chandran [Praveen_R01@infosys.com] works in the EAI practice of Infosys Technologies Ltd., focusing on platforms and technologies such as TIBCO, Vitria, and web services/BPEL.

Yves Coene [Yves.Coene@spacebel.be] currently works for SpaceBel SA in Brussels as Project Manager. He has 15 years of experience in aerospace software projects such as Ariane 5, the International Space Station, F16 MLU, and various other projects for the European Space Agency. Since 2001, he and his team have been responsible for the SSE project for ESA in Frascati, Italy.

Kevin Geminiuc [kgeminiuc@yahoo.com] currently works as a senior software architect in Denver. Over the last 15 years, Kevin has worked as a systems architect, technical manager, developer, and hardware engineer. Kevin's technical interests include SOA, RFID, AVL, and genetic software. Kevin contributed Chapter 4 for this book.

Matjaž B. Jurič [matjaz.juric@uni-mb.si] holds a Ph.D. in computer and information science, and serves as a content developer and consultant for the BPEL and SOA consulting company BPELmentor.com. He is the author of the book *Business Process Execution Language for Web Services* from Packt Publishing (ISBN: 1-904811-18-3). He is also the co-author of *J2EE Design Patterns Applied, Professional J2EE EAI, Professional EJB,* and *NET Serialization Handbook,* and has contributed to *Web Services Journal, Java Developer's Journal,* and other publications. Matjaž B. Jurič worked on Chapter 8.

The Hoa Nguyen [the.hoa.nguyen@spacebel.be] currently works for the SDC subsidiary of SpaceBel SA in Brussels as senior software engineer. His main interests are J2EE, web services, and workflow development with BPEL. Since 2001, he has been one of the lead engineers of the SSE project team at SpaceBel and is also in charge of SSE software releases and on-site SSE software installations at ESA. The Hoa Nguyen and Yves Coene contributed Chapter 3.

Arun Poduval [Arun_P@infosys.com] also works in the EAI practice of Infosys Technologies Ltd., specializing in similar technologies. Praveen Chandran and and Arun Poduval worked together on Chapter 1.

Lawrence Pravin [Lawrence.Pravin@SierraAtlantic.com] is the Product Manager, Process Integration Packs, Sierra Atlantic Inc. Process Integration Packs deliver end-to-end business process integration solutions between enterprise applications. He has over 10 years of rich experience in packaged applications, and has deep integration expertise with Oracle, PeopleSoft, Siebel, and SAP applications. Lawrence Pravin worked on Chapter 2 for this book.

Jerry Thomas [jthomas@centerstonesoft.com] is Chief Architect at CenterStone Software, which helps many of the world's largest organizations automate and manage their real estate, facilities, personnel, assets, leases, and workplace operations more efficiently. Thomas focuses on CenterStone's enterprise workplace management product and web services, BPEL, and system infrastructure. Prior to CenterStone, Thomas worked as a consultant and held principal development positions at Riverton, ONTOS, and Hewlett-Packard. Jerry Thomas wrote Chapter 6 for this cookbook.

Doug Todd [dtodd@enterrasolutions.com] is CTO of Enterra Solutions in Yardley, PA. He has more than 20 years of experience in systems architecture, applications architecture, systems integration, and applications integration with major corporations. Todd is responsible for Enterra's overall IT strategy and tactical implementation, enterprise information architecture, and technology product offerings. Doug Todd worked on Chapter 5.

Foreword

When we started Collaxa and started talking about web-service orchestration, some people wondered if we were a technology company or a music band.

Now, six years later, a wide majority of people are convinced that application development and integration have evolved from the art of writing code to the art of assembling a set of services into new business capabilities.

The standards necessary to publish and assemble services have also matured. One of the most interesting ones is BPEL (Business Process Execution Language), which was born from the fusion of XLANG and WSFL and has now been submitted to OASIS where Oracle, SAP, and more than 150 other vendors are contributing to its development.

We have had the chance over the last three years to work side by side with some of the most advanced adopters of SOA. Some customers see SOA as a way to dramatically reduce the cost and complexity of integration. Some customers see SOA as the enabler of a new class of composite metadata-driven applications, which deliver unprecedented level of flexibility and customization. All of them have, through the early adoption of the standards and tools, learned a lot about the do's and don'ts associated with the successful planning, delivery, and on-going maintenance of SOA initiatives.

This book is the fruit of those hands-on learning experiences, and I would like to thank on the behalf of Oracle all the people who have agreed to spend the time and energy necessary to share that knowledge with you.

- Edwin Khodabakchian

Vice President of Product Development at Oracle Corporation responsible for the development of Oracle BPEL Process Manager. Previously CEO and co-founder of Collaxa, a company that pioneered the web-service orchestration space and delivered the first and most comprehensive implementation of the BPEL standard. Collaxa was acquired by Oracle in June 2004.

Table of Contents

Dismantling SOA Hype: A Real-World Perspective

Service-Oriented Architecture (SOA) is attracting a lot of buzz from every realm of the IT industry. Propelled by standards-based technologies like XML, web services, and SOAP, SOA is quickly moving from pilot projects to mainstream applications critical to business operations. One of the key standards accelerating the adoption of SOA is Business Process Execution Language for web services (BPEL). BPEL was created to address the requirements of composition of web services in a service-oriented environment. In the past two years, BPEL has effectively become the most significant standard to elevate the visibility of SOA from IT to business level. BPEL is not only commoditizing the integration market, but it is also offering organizations a whole new level of agility—the ability to rapidly change applications as per changing business landscape. BPEL enables organizations to automate their business processes by orchestrating services within and across the firewall. It forces organizations to think in terms of services. Existing functionality is exposed as services. New applications are composed using services. Communication with external vendors and partners is done through services. Services are reused across different applications. Services everywhere!

New technology, after being adopted by "technology enthusiasts" and "visionaries" is adopted by "pragmatists". Similarly, after proving its worth, SOA is breaking into the mainstream. Technology Acceptance Model is one of the most influential models to explain the process of technology adoption. According to TAM, SOA has to prove itself on two terms—perceived usefulness and perceived ease of use—for SOA to successfully cross the chasm and be adopted more widely. We think SOA has proven its effectiveness on both these fronts. Not only can SOA deliver on its promises of reusability and agility (usefulness) but it can also reduce the overall cost of ownership through the standards-based approach (ease of use). That is precisely the reason why SOA enables organizations to cut the cost of IT dramatically and use the resulting savings in building other innovations.

XML, SOAP, web services, and BPEL are basic artifacts of any SOA application. In the *Business Process Execution Language for Web Services* book (Packt Publishing, October 2004, ISBN 1-904811-18-3) by Matjaž Jurič, we learned about the building blocks and how these technologies could be used to build a simple SOA solution. As organizations increase their SOA footprint, IT Managers, Architects, and developers are starting to realize that the impact of SOA on IT and business operations can be immense. After having gained confidence with web services, they want to take it to the next level. However, adopters are challenged with some basic questions: *How do I SOA-enable my existing integration investment? Can I build flexible and agile business processes? How can I administer my SOA environment without spending fortune?* There have been various best practices defined around SOA. However, missing from the map is the real-world flavor. People want to learn from people. The IT community is looking for real-world examples; examples to gain an understanding of how other companies are embarking on an SOA initiative and apply industry learning to their projects.

This book is not just another SOA best-practices manual providing generic recommendations. It is actually a best practice cookbook. You might wonder, "Why are they calling this a 'cookbook'?" *After having been exposed to different ingredients (BPEL, WSDL, and web services), this book takes the adventure to the next level by helping you cook new recipes (SOA applications) using efficient kitchen techniques (best practices). Recipes and techniques help cook food faster. And we plan do this using real-life scenario: real stories from real adopters!* 10 SOA practitioners have gotten together to share their SOA best practices and provide practical viewpoints to tackle many of the common problems SOA promises to solve. Their recommendations are based on projects in production; their existing projects could be your next ones. This book will help you learn through proven best practices and accelerate the progress of your SOA implementation.

The Structure of this Book

While talking to different companies at various stages of the SOA implementation cycle, we realized one common pattern: all SOA initiatives were driven by a business need. As you start reading this book, you will be exposed to various business challenges faced by the organizations and how companies are leveraging SOA technologies to address them. Since you are reading this book, we think that there is a business need behind your investigation and curiosity. Whether it is the need to provide a 360-degree view of the customer or to reduce the time to market, we feel that business necessity should drive SOA initiatives and justify your investment in SOA. Hence, we ensured that every chapter we present in this book is tied to a specific business use case. By ensuring this business relevance, we want to drive home the point that SOA success, to a large extent, depends on the business sponsorship and desire to address a specific business problem.

SOA is rapidly emerging technology. However, there is some level of fear and anxiety among the IT community about SOA. Is SOA real? Do I need SOA? How is it done? Hence, when we started thinking about the strategy to organize the contents of this book, we decided to take an approach of "*inspire and equip*", as shown in the following figure:

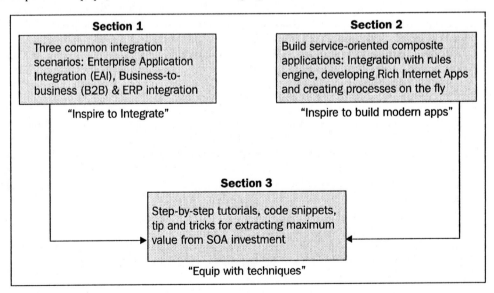

The first two sections of the book will "*inspire*" you. You will be happy to know that SOA is a reality; it exists and you can do it as well. It will encourage you to take a plunge into the world of services and test-drive SOA yourself. If you are already amidst an SOA implementation, these sections will offer you fresh insight into your current approach to deal with specific business challenges and guide you with "best practices" architecture.

In the third section, we "*equip*" you with techniques to build a better SOA application. These techniques are best practices and code snippets ranging from development to administration of an SOA application. They are generic enough to be applied in any of your existing projects, and will help you reap more benefits from your SOA implementation.

Section 1: Service-Oriented Integration

Integration has long been a thorn in the flesh of any company. Whether you attribute it to the proprietary nature of the integration products or to the cost of procuring, implementing, and maintaining these products, integration has been dreaded by the IT community. SOA promises to alleviate this everyday problem by introducing a simple concept: don't integrate applications, rather integrate services. This combined with a standards-based approach lowers the total cost of ownership. It represents the sweet spot for SOA investment. Organizations are leveraging SOA to solve a variety of everyday integration problems, thereby making SOA a mainstream technology. In the first section, we introduce different SOA integration scenarios to *inspire* integration architects and developers.

Chapter 1: Extending Enterprise Application Integration: This chapter focuses on very common business problem i.e. siloed applications and segregated data glued together using proprietary integration solution. How can we best leverage SOA to add value on top of existing integration infrastructure? By service-enabling existing data-integration processes, business processes could be easily automated by orchestrating underlying services. Infosys, a leading systems integrator, has helped many of its customers leverage their existing EAI investment, and explains you how to do exactly this. This chapter takes an example of broken customer data synchronization between Siebel and SAP, and outlines a strategy to automate this process by integrating with proprietary integration solutions like TIBCO and webMethods.

Chapter 2: Service-Oriented ERP Integration: Driven by the business requirements of different departments, countries, and subsidiaries, many organizations end up with multiple ERP systems. The result is data fragmentation and manual processes. This, in turn, leads to poor customer service and loss of revenue. The problem is how to address this problem without re-architecting the entire solution. Sierra Atlantic, a leading consulting firm specializing in integration technologies, encountered a similar issue with its client. In this chapter, Lawrence Pravin, Architect at Sierra Atlantic, takes an example of a broken sales order creation process. He walks you through a step-by-step approach to automate it across PeopleSoft HR and Oracle E-Business Suite using BPEL in a service-oriented approach.

Chapter 3: Building the Service Value Chain: Not all integrations are limited within the enterprise. Processes interact with applications, people, and partners. You might have heard the term Business-to-Business (B2B) frequently in the past few years. How can organizations build a network of services spanning multiple organizations? The European Space Agency built such a network of web services across more than 20 partners in nine different countries. The primary purpose of this network is to offer Earth Observation and Geographic Information System services to consumers. This chapter presents an initial strategy of how to architect and design a service-oriented partner-friendly network using web services and BPEL for orchestration. The focus is on four important aspects of network design: defining partner relationships, enabling partner provisioning, offering a central registry of available services, and empowering partners and end users.

Section 2: Building Modern Applications

SOA represents an evolution in the way applications are architected and built. Functions, objects, and modules were some of the artifacts used to build applications in the 90s. In essence, SOA has captured many of the old architectures and refined them to provide a new approach in building applications to meet modern business needs. Modern businesses demand faster response time i.e. the ability to meet new business requirements as fast as possible in the most economical way. Modern applications are built with these requirements in mind. Composite Application Development, Service-Oriented Development of Applications (SODA), and Agile Programming are different but related paradigms of building such modern applications in an "incremental" fashion. This second section continues the charter to *inspire* architects (this time application architects) to build modern service-oriented applications.

Chapter 4: A Services-Oriented Approach to Business Rules Development: Organizations have processes, and processes have rules. Processes need to be automated. Rules need to be defined intuitively. BPEL automates process and a rules engine automates policies. These rules essentially drive the processes. IT organizations have so far struggled to delineate business processes from rules, leading to operational inconsistency and duplication. Policy Studies Inc. provides an approach to segregate rules from processes, and offers a blueprint to expose rules as services for building cleaner applications. Using BPEL and a rules engine, PSI has built a shared services platform to perform Medicare eligibility processing for different states. Kevin Geminiuc, former Architect at PSI, explains the development strategy to integrate BPEL with a rules engine resulting in a solution that is more agile and flexible. With this approach, it is possible to change a business process without touching policies. Policies can be changed graphically without affecting the business processes.

Chapter 5: Building Rich Internet Applications for Workflow and Process Monitoring: As we discussed before, processes interact with applications, people, and partners. How can we build an application that enables business users to interact with processes seamlessly? Applications should be built to enhance end-user experience. Enterra Solutions marries the world of SOA with the world of Web 2.0. In this chapter, Doug Todd, CTO of Enterra, presents a strategy to extend BPEL workflow in a rich user interface and build an application that not only automates processes, but also ups the ante in terms of aesthetic appeal. It also represents a unique approach to customize a platform, which is SOA ready.

Chapter 6: Building BPEL Process on the Fly: BPEL provides an opportunity to bring business and IT together. Business can help define the key processes, and IT provides the necessary infrastructure to run and automate those processes. Some might argue that BPEL is too technical to be handed over to analysts for process modeling. CenterStone software, a provider of workplace management solution, addressed this very concern by building a custom designer geared towards property managers to define processes for workplace management. CenterStone devised an approach to convert the processes designed using the custom designer into BPEL processes. This chapter will *inspire* you to build applications, which will facilitate tighter integration with your business counterparts. Jerry Thomas, Chief Architect at CenterStone Software, takes you into the guts of this approach by explaining how process definition can be stored in the database and how XQuery and Saxon parser can help you to build an executable BPEL process from its higher-level process definition.

Section 3: SOA Techniques

By now, it is our sincere hope that integration and application architects are "inspired" to take on the SOA challenge. All the learning and encouragement might have invigorated you to apply SOA in your IT environment. However, as you start implementing SOA, you will need to "equip" yourself with best practices, which facilitate efficiency in design, development, and management of your SOA implementation. Best practices will accelerate your path to SOA success and help deliver on the traditional SOA promises, i.e. promote reusability by leveraging existing investment or increase business agility through flexible business processes. In this section, peers will offer you tips and tricks that add value in different stages of your implementation. This third section introduces you to four such "best practices" to derive maximum benefit from your investment. The step-by-step guides attempt to make it easy for you to adopt these proven techniques.

Chapter 7: Making BPEL Processes Dynamic: The benefit of agility has been belabored exhaustively in the industry. We decided to go back to basics and offer you a very simple technical insight into how SOA enables business agility. Agility is directly correlated to the ability to quickly respond to business changes. By using dynamic partner links, processes can effectively change their behavior to adapt themselves to external business conditions and thereby offer flexibility. SPS Commerce, provider of hosted EDI solutions, has built an SOA-enabled platform for enabling seamless exchange of EDI documents between different entities. In this chapter, SPS Commerce will explain the significance of dynamic partner links and walk you through a step-by-step guide to implement partner links in a sample loan-processing scenario. This approach will enable you to quickly add/delete service providers participating in a business process without actually changing the process.

Chapter 8: Using WSIF for Integration: Organizations operate in a heterogeneous environment. Applications are built using different technologies, from different vendors and different implementers. As you start building a process, you will realize that the underlying applications are not necessarily web services. More often than not, they are either .NET applications or applications built using J2EE, i.e. either purchased applications or home-grown Java Applications. Matjaž Jurič, author of the Packt book *Business Process Execution Language for Web Services* (ISBN: 1-904811-18-3) presents a strategy to integrate with Java resources using Web Services Invocation Framework (WSIF). Matjaž, professor of Computer Science at the University of Maribor, argues that although it is possible to expose these applications as web services and use them in the process, accessing these resources natively can improve the application performance significantly.

Chapter 9: BPEL with Reliable Processing: The success of any service in the SOA world depends upon its degree of reusability, which in turn depends upon the quality of service offered. As you run your SOA applications, many things could go wrong. Network connections may be lost, participating applications may go down, incoming data might be corrupted, etc. These external interruptions can degrade the quality of a particular application. How can you design an application that can withstand all these failures and still emerge as a winner? Qualcomm encountered this specific issue while leveraging SOA to build the *Entitlement Provisioning* application. Presented in the fashion of step-by-step tutorial, Jeremy Bolie, IT Manager, and Michael Cardella, Architect at Qualcomm, share with you a strategy to design a reusable BPEL process capable of offering any service and defeating rectifiable errors.

Chapter 10: Managing a BPEL Production Environment: The last chapter in this cookbook deals with an important aspect of any application—maintenance. More dollars are spent in maintenance and enhancement of an application than the combined amount spent during its design, development, and testing phases. Once the application is deployed into production, the real work begins. Belgacom, one of the leading telecommunications companies in Belgium, has automated DSL service provisioning and diagnosis using BPEL. Having been in production for a long time, Belgacom has vast practical experience in managing a BPEL infrastructure. In this chapter, Stany Blanvalet, former Architect at Belgacom, explains various strategies for managing a BPEL production environment. This is a must read for all the BPEL administrators.

Conclusion

Having progressed from "inspire" to "equip" mission, we are confident that you will have a strong real-world perspective of how SOA is put in use. Each of these chapters brings into focus a real-world business issue and offers how a specific company has approached SOA to address that issue. This does not necessarily mean that this is the *only* best solution for the problem at hand. It is just one of the many solutions. However, after reading through these chapters, you will realize that your business environment might be similar and some (possibly all) ideas presented in a specific chapter are applicable to your situation. Some may require modification; some may be applied directly! If you are able to relate to at least one of the 10 business issues presented here and apply some of the strategies presented in this book, we have achieved what we set out to do.

Best of luck with your SOA journey! Enjoy the ride! Carpe Diem!

Conventions

In this book, you will find a number of styles of text that distinguish between different kinds of information. Here are some examples of these styles, and an explanation of their meaning.

There are three styles for code. Code words in text are shown as follows: "We can include other contexts through the use of the include directive."

A block of code will be set as follows:

```
WhereCondition where = WhereConditionHelper.whereInstancesStale();
    IInstanceHandle[] instances = getLocator(domainId,
domainPassword).listInstances(where);
        for(int i=0; i<instances.length; i++){
            instances[i].delete();
    }
```

When we wish to draw your attention to a particular part of a code block, the relevant lines or items will be made bold:

```
WhereCondition where = WhereConditionHelper.whereInstancesStale();
    IInstanceHandle[] instances = getLocator(domainId,
domainPassword).listInstances(where);
        for(int i=0; i<instances.length; i++){
            instances[i].delete();
    }
```

New terms and **important words** are introduced in a bold-type font. Words that you see on the screen, in menus or dialog boxes for example, appear in our text like this: "clicking the Next button moves you to the next screen".

> Warnings or important notes appear in a box like this.

Tips and tricks appear like this.

Reader Feedback

Feedback from our readers is always welcome. Let us know what you think about this book, what you liked or may have disliked. Reader feedback is important for us to develop titles that you really get the most out of.

To send us general feedback, simply drop an email to feedback@packtpub.com, making sure to mention the book title in the subject of your message.

If there is a book that you need and would like to see us publish, please send us a note in the SUGGEST A TITLE form on www.packtpub.com or email suggest@packtpub.com.

If there is a topic that you have expertise in and you are interested in either writing or contributing to a book, see our author guide on www.packtpub.com/authors.

Customer Support

Now that you are the proud owner of a Packt book, we have a number of things to help you to get the most from your purchase.

Downloading the Code for the Book

Visit http://www.packtpub.com/support, and select this book from the list of titles to download any example code or extra resources for this book. The files available for download will then be displayed.

> The downloadable files contain instructions on how to use them.

Errata

Although we have taken every care to ensure the accuracy of our contents, mistakes do happen. If you find a mistake in one of our books—maybe a mistake in text or code—we would be grateful if you would report this to us. By doing this you can save other readers from frustration, and help to improve subsequent versions of this book. If you find any errata, report them by visiting http://www.packtpub.com/support, selecting your book, clicking on the Submit Errata link, and entering the details of your errata. Once your errata have been verified, your submission will be accepted and the errata added to the list of existing errata. The existing errata can be viewed by selecting your title from http://www.packtpub.com/support.

Questions

You can contact us at questions@packtpub.com if you are having a problem with some aspect of the book, and we will do our best to address it.

1

Extending Enterprise Application Integration

by Praveen Chandran and Arun Poduval

Leverage the orchestration capability of Oracle BPEL Process Manager to enable standards-based business process integration that complements traditional EAI middleware.

Most organizations have a highly disparate application infrastructure comprising a variety of applications from multiple vendors, running on different platforms, and created with completely different technologies. Traditional **Enterprise Application Integration (EAI)** products—from companies such as TIBCO, webMethods, Vitria, and SeeBeyond—have emerged in the last decade to tackle these integration challenges. Over the last few years, many organizations have made significant investments in these EAI solutions. As a result, business integrations in the EAI space tend to be locked into a single vendor, and the integration components are tightly coupled.

The cost of maintaining these proprietary integration links is a significant burden. Specialized skills are required, exacerbating the cost and stability concerns. Furthermore, ripping and replacing existing EAI solutions is not a plausible alternative for an organization protecting massive investments in EAI.

BPEL addresses all these problems by delivering a standards-based, platform-neutral solution. The loosely coupled BPEL process eliminates vendor lock-in, reduces integration costs, and provides interoperability; it also adds a sophisticated layer of security, exception management, and logging. Most important, companies can leverage their existing infrastructure, service-enable it, and orchestrate it using BPEL.

In this installment of *The BPEL Cookbook*, we will present an architectural blueprint for leveraging Oracle BPEL Process Manager to develop new integration solutions as well as interface with existing ones. It includes a case study in which orchestrated web services must be integrated with existing heterogeneous EAI solutions based on TIBCO BusinessWorks and webMethods.

Furthermore, because any business process implementation is incomplete without a carefully designed error management, security, and logging framework, we'll explain how BPEL scopes and compensation handlers can make this process more robust and fault-tolerant, as well as how to secure the BPEL process and participating services.

Case Study Background

EAI is an excellent driver for service-enabling existing applications; existing middleware processes can be exposed as web services, which are then orchestrated via BPEL.

The following diagram illustrates a generic approach in which Oracle BPEL Process Manager is used to orchestrate existing EAI interfaces as well as to integrate new applications. This approach assumes that the middleware can expose the business processes as web services and that the application servers themselves have web service interfaces.

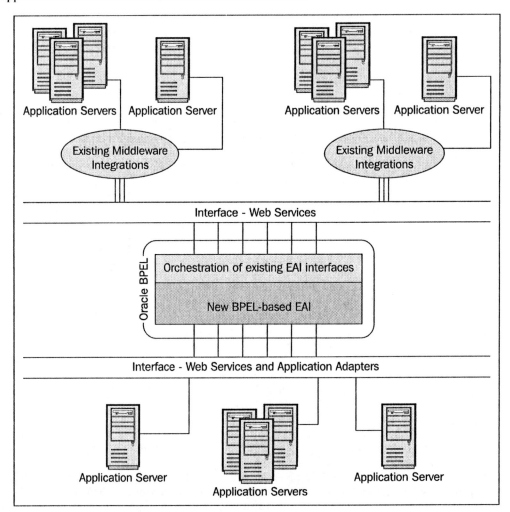

An analysis of a specific case study involving two traditional EAI middleware products demonstrates how BPEL can play an important role in integrating the two products.

In many organizations, changes made in one customer "system of record" are not propagated to the other systems in which customer data is maintained. Consider a scenario in which an enterprise, for various business reasons, ends up using two middleware products from different vendors, such as Siebel CRM integrated with TIBCO BusinessWorks and SAP R/3 integrated with webMethods.

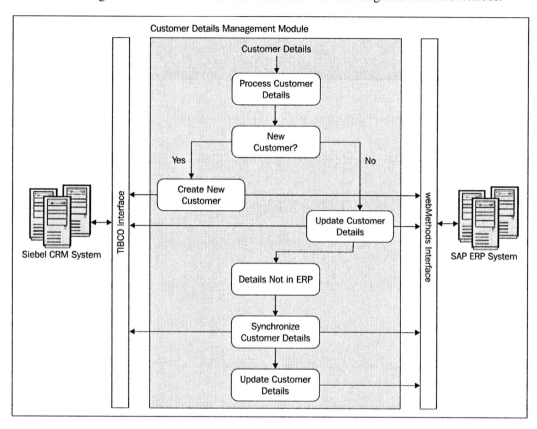

In this model, inconsistent customer data across the SAP and Siebel systems can adversely affect customer service levels and can drive down department and organization revenues. Rather, consistency can be maintained through a common Customer Details Management Module that has multiple interfacing points with the TIBCO and webMethods integrations. For example, when Siebel receives customer data, it checks whether the customer is a new or existing one, and then either adds new data to SAP or updates existing customer data in both apps.

You could use the existing middleware tools (TIBCO and webMethods) to achieve this integration, but doing so would simply increase the footprint of proprietary integration and vendor lock-in. This situation represents an excellent opportunity to service-enable the applications, thereby achieving a standards-based, vendor-agnostic solution.

The first step toward achieving a standards-based interface in EAI is to expose the process as a web service. Most middleware platforms can talk to each other through web services, but the scenario becomes complex when a set of interfacing services must be glued together with appropriate business logic.

You could use another middleware process or even complex Java code to orchestrate web services. However, the process would have to provide following capabilities:

- Parallel web service invocations
- Asynchronous web service invocations
- Loose coupling between services and portability
- Exposing the whole orchestration with standards-based interfaces
- Orchestration monitoring

As shown in the following figure, a prefabricated standards-based orchestration solution based on BPEL can address these issues:

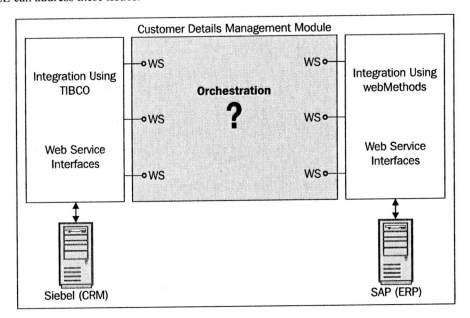

Introducing BPEL into this scenario has the following potential advantages:

- BPEL supports loosely coupled web service orchestration.
- Business logic (even parallel flows!) can be represented in simple XML tags.
- Data can be easily routed among services with simple assign (copy rules) and invoke statements.

- The Customer Details Management Module can be invoked as an independent web service component from another orchestration, middleware tool, or web application.
- Processes can be managed via a simple GUI, such as with Oracle BPEL Process Manager.

Most middleware tools can expose their business processes as web services, making it easier to bridge existing integrations with BPEL orchestrations. In fact, you can use a common message format for all the middleware service interfaces involved.

Now let's consider how Oracle BPEL Process Manager can be used to achieve this synchronization of customer data across SAP and Siebel.

Implementing the Customer Details Management Module

BPEL plays an instrumental role in automating the customer data synchronization process between SAP and Siebel. The steps involved in implementing this BPEL process are:

1. Expose TIBCO and webMethods processes as web services.
2. Orchestrate web services using a BPEL process.
3. Add exception-management capability to the BPEL process.
4. Secure communication between Oracle BPEL Process Manager, application adapters, and the EAI tool.
5. Centralize the logging and notification process.

Step 1: Expose TIBCO and webMethods Processes as Web Services

Customer information is represented in a canonical format and contains fields needed for both SAP and Siebel. If you're passing this generic format across TIBCO and webMethods, these platforms will convert the canonical format into Siebel and SAP customer records, respectively.

Here are the steps you would take to expose the BusinessWorks process as a web service:

1. Analyze the functionality offered by your BusinessWorks process, to determine whether it can be an independent component in the integration scenario.
2. Determine the input and output of the process.
3. If input and output are complex, use W3C XML schemas (XSDs) to define them. You can use XSDs to define your custom fault schema as well.
4. Create the WSDL, using the WSDL palette, and define input and output message formats (associate them with predefined XSDs, if required). You can import existing WSDL as well.
5. Configure an HTTP Connection resource.

6. Use a SOAP Event Source as the first activity, followed by business logic, and then use a SOAP Send Reply to expose the process as a service.

7. Associate the HTTP Connection resource with the Event Source.

8. Associate WSDL and Send Reply with the Event Source.

9. Handle possible exceptions, and use SOAP Send Fault for sending exceptions to the service client.

10. If your machine name is mymachine, the port used for the HTTP Connection resource is 8000, and the process name is SOAPService, your service can be accessed using the URL http://mymachine:8000/SOAPService.

11. Get the final WSDL of the service from the WSDL tab of the Event Source activity.

Here's how you would do the same with webMethods:

1. Check whether your webMethods Flow Service can be an independent component in the integration scenario.

2. Specify Execute ACL to Anonymous under the Permissions tab if you want to invoke this web service from outside the webMethods environment without any authentication.

3. Select the Flow Service in webMethods Developer, and click on Generate WSDL from the Tools menu.

4. While generating the WSDL document, specify the protocol (SOAP-RPC/SOAP-MSG/HTTP-GET/HTTP-POST) and transport mechanism (HTTP/HTTPS).

5. Define the target namespace for the WSDL document.

6. Enter the IP address or name of the machine where webMethods Integration Server is hosted in the Host field.

7. In the Port field, enter the port number to be used for connecting to the current Integration Server.

8. Save the WSDL document to the local file system. You can find the service endpoint in the generated WSDL document.

---

webMethods Integration Server sends predefined SOAP faults for certain error conditions. If you have to send custom SOAP faults, you should use a custom SOAP processor. You should also use a wrapper service or a custom SOAP processor to expose the service as a document/literal web service.

Now, suppose you have the following three TIBCO web services (implemented with TIBCO BusinessWorks processes and TIBCO Adapter for Siebel):

- Siebel Add
- Siebel Update
- Siebel Query

Similarly, you have the following webMethods web services deployed (using webMethods Integration Server and webMethods SAP R/3 Adapter):

- SAP Add
- SAP Update

The solution architecture can be summarized as follows:

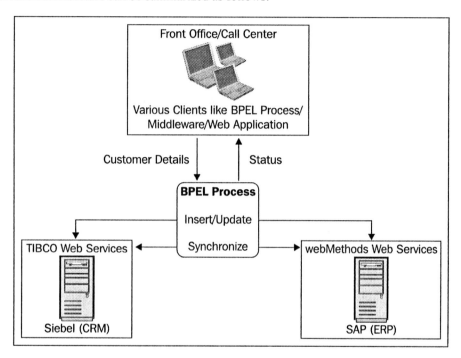

As seen in the figure, the BPEL process brokers the conversation between the front-office call center and back-end SAP and Siebel CRM applications via EAI tools.

Here are some best practices for exposing middleware processes as web services:

- Adhere to WS-I standards whenever possible.
- Try to expose services in "document" style with literal encoding. If that option is not available, use "RPC" style with literal encoding. Although either is recommended by WS-I, you will find document style easier, at least when you create copy rules for a BPEL assign activity—with RPC style, all the schema elements come as separate message parts, whereas with document style, the entire message is delivered in one part. You can use a single copy rule to copy the entire schema, thereby easing the development effort, and verify the style and encoding in the final WSDL document.

- Avoid the use of SOAP encoding; the SOAP Action attribute of WSDL is an empty string.
- Confirm that the middleware uses WSDL 1.1 to describe the interface of the web service.
- Use HTTP binding of SOAP.
- Make sure that all XSDs used for describing the schema conform to the XML schema specification proposed by the W3C. For example, global element declarations should not use references to other global elements; that is, use the type attribute instead of the ref attribute.

Step 2: Orchestrate Web Services

Having exposed middleware processes as web services, you can then orchestrate them using Oracle BPEL Process Manager, which has a powerful, GUI-based BPEL-authoring interface.

Previously, we mentioned that an important aspect of the Customer Details Management Module is that it synchronizes customer data between SAP and Siebel. This process is visually created in BPEL Designer as shown in the following figure:

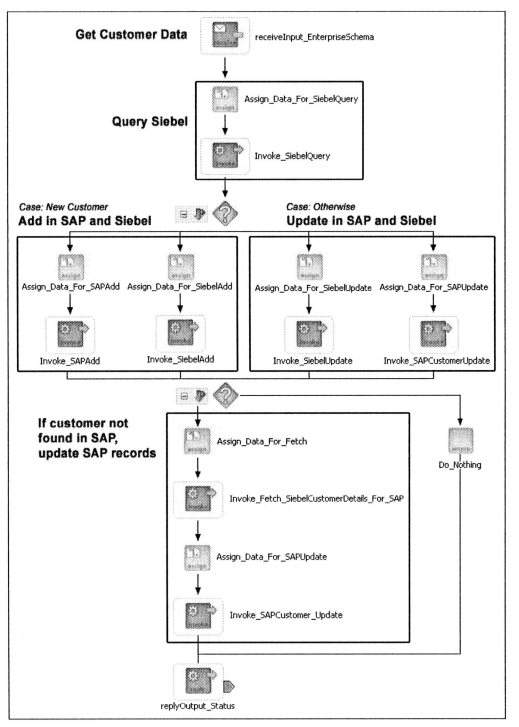

The BPEL Processes Images in this chapter have been edited for clarity purposes. Actual BPEL process will look slightly different in BPEL Designer (Partners Links are not shown in this BPEL process).

Here's a summary of this process flow:

1. A receive activity accepts the customer details (enterprise schema).

2. Details are passed to Siebel through assign and invoke (Siebel Query service) activities.

3. Via a pick activity, the Siebel Query result is used to determine whether the customer is existing or new.

4. If the customer is new, parallel execution is invoked, with flow activity adding the customer in both Siebel and SAP; otherwise, another parallel flow updates customer details in both applications.

5. If the customer details are not present in SAP, those fields are fetched from Siebel by Siebel Query. This and the other SAP fields to be updated are passed to SAP Update, possibly via a set of assign copy rules.

6. The final status of Customer Update/Addition is returned by use of an explicit reply activity.

As you can see, on either side of the business process are web services for adding and updating Siebel and SAP data. These web services, which we designed in Step 1, internally invoke EAI processes.

This BPEL process addresses the business requirements of customer management, but it still can't handle exceptions. For example, what would happen if a customer was added successfully in Siebel but addition failed in SAP? To address that issue, you need to enable exception management in your business process.

Step 3: Add Exception Management Capability

Exception management allows a BPEL process to handle error messages or other exceptions returned by outside web services and to generate error messages in response to business or run-time faults.

The following table contains exceptions that need to be handled to make the customer management BPEL process more robust.

No.	Case	Resolution
Case 1	Siebel Query fails	Terminate the process; retry
Case 2	Siebel Add fails; SAP Add succeeds	Compensate to remove SAP record; retry
Case 3	Siebel Add succeeds; SAP Add fails	Normal flow; retry
Case 4	Siebel Add fails; SAP Add fails	Normal flow; retry
Case 5	Siebel Update succeeds; SAP Update fails	Normal flow; retry
Case 6	Siebel Update fails; SAP Update succeeds	Compensate to roll back SAP record; retry
Case 7	Siebel Update fails; SAP Update fails	Normal flow; retry

Cases other than 1, 2, and 6 (discussed later) needn't be handled explicitly to keep the data consistent.

It is necessary to track the status of the web service to catch exceptions and take appropriate actions. Before a discussion of how cases 1, 2, and 6 are handled, let's see how the status of a specific web service is tracked.

The entire BPEL process has these reply schema attributes:

- `Siebel_Add_Status`
- `Siebel_Update_Status`
- `SAP_Add_Status`
- `SAP_Update_Status`

All these attributes can have the values `Failed`, `Success`, or `NA`, which can be set by the BPEL process at various points. To set the `Failed` status, the process can catch the SOAP faults thrown by target web services (use a catch handler with each `invoke` activity). The client invoking the Customer Details Management Module can resend the details in case of any failures.

Now, let's see how exceptions are managed:

Case 1

If the Siebel query itself fails, the process should be terminated, and the invoking client can retry.

Case 2

When customer-details insertion fails in Siebel and succeeds in SAP (they occur in parallel), data consistency will be lost. Moreover, in the case of a retry, the following problems may occur:

- If you try to invoke the BPEL process to insert customer details into Siebel, customer details may be duplicated in SAP.
- If you try to invoke the BPEL process to update customer details, update in Siebel will fail, because there is no corresponding record.

To handle the situation, you have to delete the SAP customer record before a retry takes place, using another webMethods web service with a BPEL compensation handler and scopes.

The scope and compensate activities are key BPEL development tools. A *scope* is a container and context for other activities; a *scope activity* is analogous to a {} block in a programming language. A scope simplifies the BPEL flow by grouping functional structures, and provides handlers for faults, events, and compensation as well as data variables and correlation sets.

Oracle BPEL Process Manager provides two constructs for handling compensation:

- **Compensation handler**: This handler is the business logic for achieving rollbacks. Handlers can be defined for processes and scopes.
- **Compensate activity**: This activity invokes the compensation handler on an inner scope activity that has already successfully completed, and it can be invoked only from within a fault handler or another compensation handler.

Exceptions are caught at the scope level via catch handlers. Catch handlers, in turn, use the compensate activity to invoke the compensation handler for the inner scope. The compensation handler will perform the required rollbacks.

Returning to our example, let's assume that our BPEL process has two scopes: an inner one and an outer one. Invoke activities for SAP Add and Siebel Add services come under outer scope, but only SAP Add comes under the inner scope. A compensation handler can be associated with the inner scope, and the compensation handler will contain an invoke activity for the SAP Delete service.

You have to associate a catch block with the outer scope so that a `siebelAddfault` sent by the BusinessWorks web service can be caught. Whenever a `siebelAddfault` occurs, a compensate activity compensates the inner scope, and the SAP customer record is deleted. Note that compensate will be successful only if *all* the activities in the inner scope have been successful.

A modified BPEL process with scopes and compensation handlers is shown in the figure below:

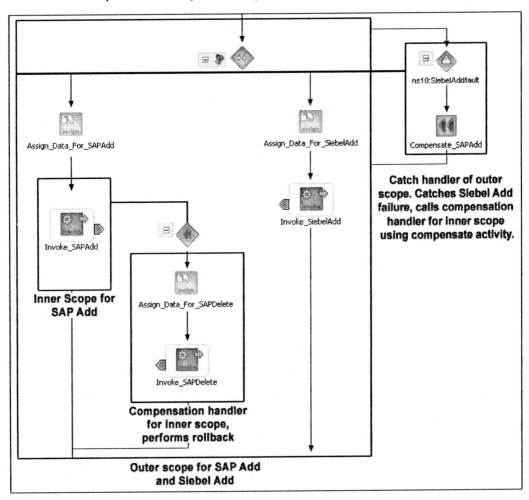

Case 6

The transaction also fails if the Siebel update fails and the SAP update succeeds. This leads to data inconsistency; thus, you have to use compensation logic to roll back the transaction that occurred in SAP. The compensation handler is associated with the SAP Update service and will invoke the SAP Rollback service. Modification of the BPEL process will adhere to the guidelines identified earlier.

The ability to explicitly invoke the compensate activity is the underpinning of the error-handling framework of BPEL. Unlike traditional EAI compensation mechanisms, BPEL offers a standardized method of dealing with rollbacks.

Having created a BPEL process to orchestrate TIBCO and webMethods web services, let's see how we can make the communication between BPEL, adapters, and EAI tools more secure.

Step 4: Secure Business Communication

Security can be enabled at two levels: outbound (invoking secure TIBCO and webMethods services) and inbound (securing the BPEL process).

Outbound Security

TIBCO and webMethods services need to be secured to prevent unauthorized access. Oracle BPEL Process Manager supports HTTP basic and WS-Security authentication for calling external services. This example focuses on how to secure the TIBCO and webMethods services and mechanisms to call them from the BPEL process, using HTTP authentication.

Web services deployed in TIBCO BusinessWorks and webMethods Integration Server support HTTP basic authentication. While designing the TIBCO web service, check the Use Basic Authentication checkbox on the Transport Details tab of the SOAP event source activity. While deploying the web service by using TIBCO Administrator, you can set service access levels for different users/roles. When designing the web service with webMethods Developer, you can set the ACL (Access Control List) for different operations.

If you use basic authentication while deploying the TIBCO and webMethods services, the services, on each invocation, will expect credentials, and these should be passed by the BPEL process. This task can be achieved by setting two "partner link" properties: httpUsername and httpPassword. The value of these properties can be set statically as follows:

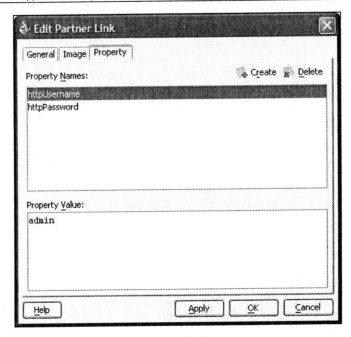

To pass the credentials dynamically, use a copy rule.

```
<copy>
   <from variable="varUsername"/>
   <to partnerLink="p1" bpelx:property="httpUsername"/>
</copy>
```

In addition, you can secure TIBCO and webMethods services by using WS-Security. BPEL processes can pass WS-Security authentication headers to WS-Security-secured web services. You need to define the WS-Security headers that the service supports in the WSDL document for the service. These header fields can then be manipulated as variables in the BPEL process, just like message-body data elements. You can find more details about WS-Security authentication in the HotelShopFlow example, downloadable from the OTN at http://www.oracle.com/technology/products/ias/bpel/files/hotelshopdemostandalone.zip.

Inbound Security

BPEL processes can be secured from invocation by unauthorized users using HTTP authentication; it is also possible to set different credentials for different BPEL processes.

To enable this security, HTTP basic authentication has to be enabled at the application-server level. Credentials can then be extracted in the BPEL process and passed to TIBCO and webMethods web services as "partner link" properties.

For more details about BPEL security, listen to the "Securing BPEL Processes & Services" Webinar on OTN.

Step 5: Centralize Logging and Error Handling

Your business processes are now secure and robust, but it is equally important to build logging and notification capability into them. Building a centralized logging and error-handling framework will make the application even more robust, increase reusability, and reduce development costs. You can build such a framework by using a web service from the BPEL process as well as from middleware. Via Oracle BPEL Process Manager, you can add logging to this service with the file adapter and require that an email notification be sent in case of error.

The following sample schema can be used for the framework:

Schema Element	Description
ROLE	Roles such as ERROR, DEBUG, WARNING, and INFO
CODE	Error code
DESCRIPTION	Error description
SOURCE	Source of error
EMAIL	Email ID to which notification has to be sent

This BPEL process can be exposed as an asynchronous one-way web service, which makes the clients of this service continue operations without any delay. The centralized logging and notification process **LogNotify** is shown in the following figure (Partners Links are not shown in this BPEL process for clarity purpose):

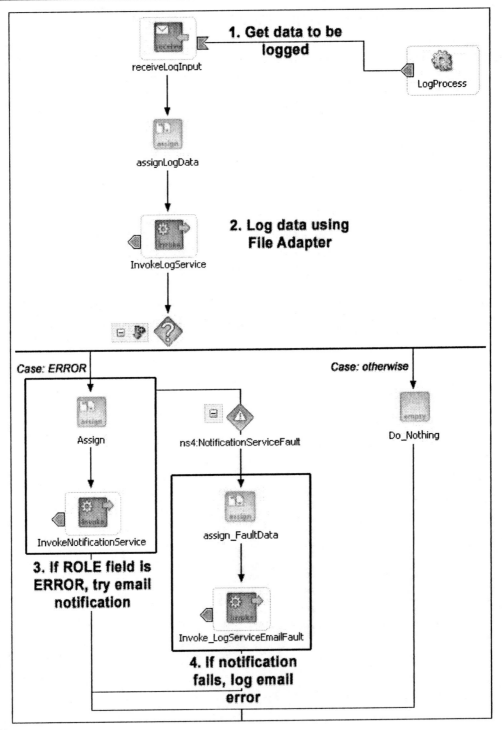

1. Get data to be logged

LogProcess

receiveLogInput

assignLogData

2. Log data using File Adapter

InvokeLogService

Case: ERROR

Case: otherwise

Assign

ns4:NotificationServiceFault

Do_Nothing

InvokeNotificationService

assign_FaultData

3. If ROLE field is ERROR, try email notification

Invoke_LogServiceEmailFault

4. If notification fails, log email error

As shown in the figure above, the LogNotify process does the following:

1. Receives information to be logged from an external process.
2. Invokes Log Service to write this data into a log file. Log Service leverages the file adapter for this purpose.
3. If logging is successful, the process completes. In addition, if the ROLE field contains ERROR, the service will notify the relevant person via email. Email information is retrieved from the original message received (see the sample schema).
4. If notification fails, the process ends after the notification error has been logged in a file.

Each invoke activity in our main BPEL process can have a separate try-catch block. SOAP faults sent by the middleware process (which may even include exceptions thrown by the end application) are handled in the catch block and routed to the common logging and error-handling framework.

The figure below shows how the LogNotify process is invoked when Siebel Add fails:

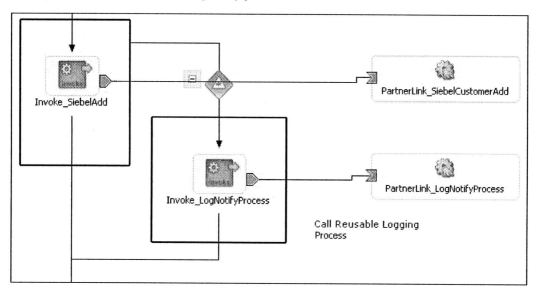

Conclusion

The integration market is flooded with powerful EAI products, with which lots of integration has already been done. BPEL represents a unique choice for service-enabling these existing EAI solutions. By exposing existing middleware processes as web services and orchestrating them with Oracle BPEL Process Manager, organizations can embark on the route of SOA.

2

Service-Oriented ERP Integration

by Lawrence Pravin

A step-by-step approach for integrating PeopleSoft 8.9 CRM with Oracle Applications 11i using BPEL.

Many organizations have heterogeneous application portfolios that cross different departments, geographic locations, or subsidiaries. While multiple ERP systems may be necessary to meet the requirements of the business unit, they essentially result in data fragmentation. Integration of these systems is complex and traditionally handled in a proprietary manner; nevertheless, companies invest significant energy in integrating information spread across multiple ERP systems to make better business decisions.

BPEL provides a standard, process-centric way to integrate disparate systems. Oracle's BPEL Process Manager, a key tool in Oracle Fusion Middleware for delivering service-oriented architecture (SOA), supports the industry-standard BPEL specification backed by Microsoft, IBM, SAP, and BEA, and is widely recognized as an enterprise blueprint for reducing the cost, complexity, and inflexibility of integration projects.

In this installment of *The BPEL Cookbook*, we'll present an approach for integrating PeopleSoft 8.9 CRM (PeopleTools 8.46) with Oracle Applications 11i using BPEL. Specifically, via a sample business scenario, you'll learn how PeopleSoft is configured to expose its modules as web services and how the BPEL Applications adapter is configured to interact with Oracle apps.

Functional Scenario

In a typical order-management business scenario, an order is entered into the CRM system, and fulfillment occurs through the back-office ERP. In this example, we are using PeopleSoft as the front-office application to manage marketing, sales, and service operations and Oracle E-Business suite for ERP (order management, inventory, and financials). The business process considered here is the **Quote-to-Order** process.

One part of this business process—quote and order entry—is executed in the CRM system, while order fulfillment is performed in the ERP system. To optimize internal operations, the entire cross-application Quote-to-Order business process needs to be automated.

Here is the functionality available in this business process integration:

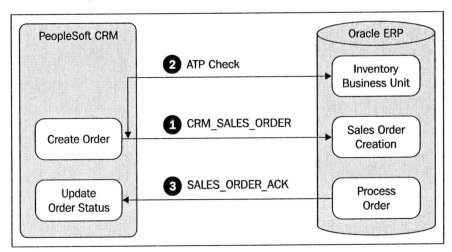

Step 1: Sales orders creation in PeopleSoft:

A sales order in PeopleSoft can be created either by converting a quote into a sales order, or directly through the Order Capture screen.

Upon submission, the system will check for the required information and change the status to "Open"; otherwise the status will be "Hold".

This sales order process will invoke and submit the order information to the Integration process. This in turn will invoke BPEL Process Manager.

BPEL Process Manager converts the messages data into the format required by the Oracle ERP Order Management module.

- The sales order creation takes place in the Oracle ERP application, and the order acknowledgment is propagated to PeopleSoft.

Step 2: ATP check in Oracle ERP:

During the order creation process, the salesperson may wish to check the availability of the material to promise the delivery date.

PeopleSoft CRM will make a synchronous call to the ERP application to get the on-hand available quantity using the Item/Product Availability inquiry component.

BPEL Process Manager will transmit this ATP check request to Oracle ERP.

Oracle ERP will check the available quantity for the specific item from the inventory. It will send back the relevant availability details to BPEL Process Manager.

- BPEL Process Manager will pass on this ATP response information to PeopleSoft CRM. Based on this operation, the customer will be promised the actual delivery date.

Step 3: Propagation of order status updates from Oracle ERP to PeopleSoft CRM:

After propagating the sales order to the ERP application, the order is booked in ERP, the acknowledgment is sent to the BPEL process, and in turn is propagated to PeopleSoft CRM system, where the order status will be changed to "In Process".

- Oracle ERP will propagate the changes to the order status from time to time. This status from ERP is mapped to equivalent status in CRM.

Here we will focus on the order creation step. The design-time viewlet at `http://www.oracle.com/ technology/pub/articles/bpel_cookbook/files/configuration_setup_viewlet_version3.0_ viewlet.html` illustrates the configuration and execution in action. For further details about other steps in this process, please refer to the *Oracle Apps Integration Cookbook* at `http://download .oracle.com/otndocs/products/integration/oracle_apps_integration_cookbook.pdf`.

Solution Overview

Now that you understand the functional business process, let's see how it's accomplished at the architecture level. The following figure provides a high-level overview of the participating components for a typical integration between PeopleSoft CRM and Oracle Applications with Oracle BPEL Process Manager as the integration platform:

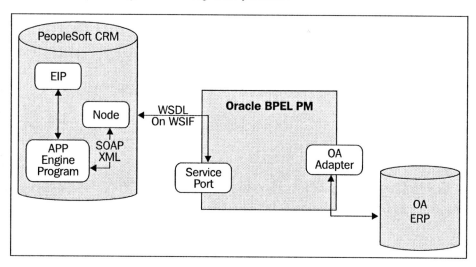

Enterprise Integration Points (EIPs) are web service connections that allow PeopleSoft applications to work smoothly with third-party systems and other PeopleSoft software. Upon submission of an order in PeopleSoft CRM, an EIP in PeopleSoft transforms it to XML format. This Order XML is then passed on to the attached PeopleCode method (WSDL_ORDER). (PeopleCode is the PeopleSoft programming language for enforcing business rules or performing other customizations.) WSDL_ORDER will convert the received Order XML into SOAP XML and will send this request to the PeopleSoft remote node. The **remote node** is what handshakes with a configured web service in BPEL Process Manager.

A web service can be invoked from PeopleSoft by mapping the remote node to the WSDL using **Web Service Invocation Framework (WSIF)** binding, which is strongly supported by BPEL Process Manager. Upon receiving this SOAP XML, the PeopleSoft node will invoke the web service based on the WSDL imported and configured to this node. The web service is invoked and executed in BPEL Process Manager.

BPEL Process Manager processes the order data as SOAP XML and sends it to Oracle Applications; it internally leverages the Oracle Applications (OA) Adapter to communicate with 11i. The OA Adapter is a pure JCA 1.5 Resource Adapter that can be used to send and receive messages from E-Business Suite. Oracle Applications exposes some of the seeded API and table to external applications via this adapter.

Oracle Applications processes the order and sends the acknowledgment; BPEL Process Manager receives this response and forwards it to the PeopleSoft node. The node will then respond to the PeopleCode that requested the web service. The latter will retrieve the XML data and submit it to the configured component interface in PeopleSoft. A **component interface** is what exposes PeopleSoft components for synchronous access from another application (written in Java or PeopleCode).

That's the high-level flow of Order data from PeopleSoft to Oracle Applications and back. In the next section, you'll learn how to expose PeopleSoft CRM modules as web services, build a BPEL process, and configure the OA Adapter.

Integrating PeopleSoft CRM with Oracle ERP

Once the order is submitted in PeopleSoft CRM, order information needs to be passed to Oracle Apps. There are three key steps in this process.

1. Design the business process in Oracle BPEL Process Manager.
2. Configure the OA Adapter.
3. Configure PeopleSoft.

Let's take a deep drive into each of these steps.

Step 1: Design the BPEL Process

In this step, we will use BPEL Designer to create a process. BPEL Process Manager will receive the SOAP XML containing sales order information from PeopleSoft and transform it to the OA Adapter's XML format. (The schema will be generated by the OA Adapter automatically when the partner link is created for the calling API.) Then, the OA Adapter partner link will be invoked and transformed and the Order XML submitted to Oracle Applications. The Oracle API will process the order and return the order number in output acknowledgment XML.

BPEL Process Manager handles remote and binding faults. When a connection is not available, it retries five times and then throws an exception. When a binding exception occurs, the binding fault will be handled.

A typical example of an integration business process designed for BPEL Process Manager is shown in the following figure (*This figure has been edited for clarity purposes. Actual BPEL process will look slightly different in BPEL Designer. Partners Links are not shown in this BPEL process*):

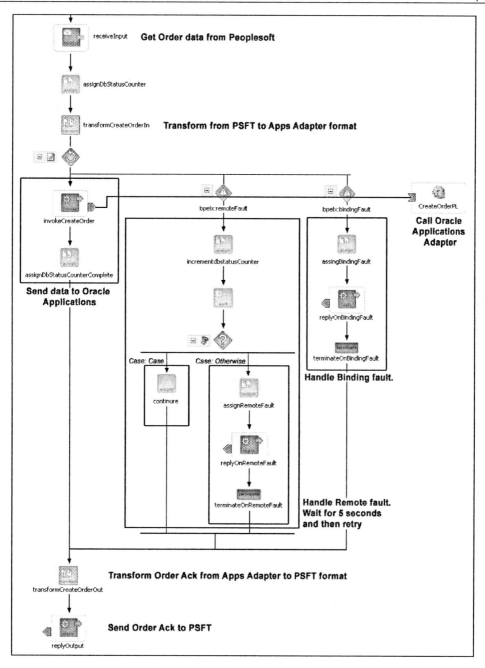

The critical activities in the process would be:

1. Select Applications | New Application Workspace | New Project | BPEL Process Project.

2. Import the schema to define the input and output variables of the BPEL process.

    a. From the structure window select project schemas | import Schema.
        Enter the input schema name (createorder.xsd).

    b. From the structure window, select Message Types.

        o Select CreateOrderRequestMessage and map the `CreateOrderIn` root element of `createorder.xsd`.

        o Select CreateOrderResponseMessage and map the `CreateOrderOut` root element of `createorder.xsd`.

    c. From the structure window, select Variables.

        o Confirm that `Inputvariable` is mapped to `CreateOrderRequestMessage`.

        o Confirm that `outputvariable` is mapped to `CreateOrderResponseMessage`.

3. Create the partner link for OA Adapter.

    a. Add a partner link activity from the component palette to the CreateOrder process and name it CreateOrderPL.

    b. Click on Define Adapter Service.

    c. Configure BPEL Process Manager and OA Adapter for the partner link (more on that in the *Step 2: Configure OA Adapter* section).

4. Add an `invoke` activity to call OA Adapter.

    a. Drag and drop the `invoke` activity to the process and double-click on it.

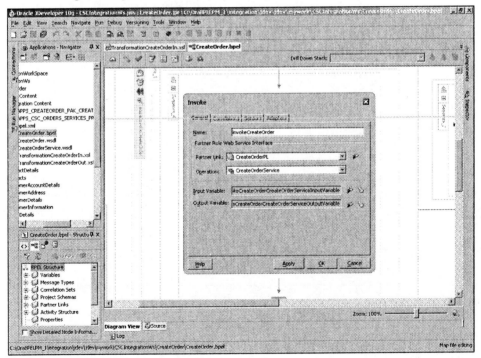

b. Map the partner link to CreateOrderPL and create the input and output variables.

5. Add a transform activity above the invoke activity for transforming PeopleSoft outbound XML to Oracle Apps inbound XML.

a. Double-click on the transform activity. Select inputVariable as Source Variable, invokeCreateOrderInputVariable as Target Variable, and click on the create mapping icon as shown:

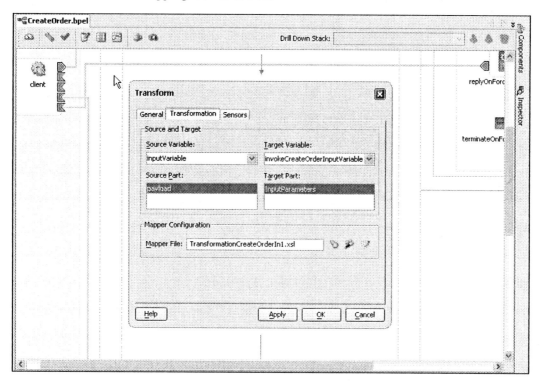

b. Map the source and target schemas as shown in the following screenshot:

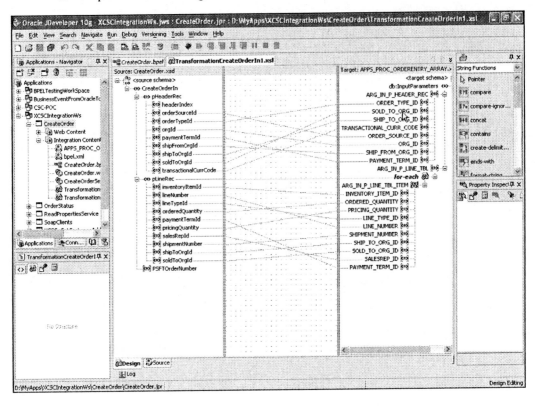

6. Add another `transform` activity below the `invoke` activity for transforming Oracle Apps outbound XML to PeopleSoft inbound XML.

    a. Double-click on the `transform` activity. Select invokeCreateOrderOutputVariable as Source Variable, outputVariable as Target Variable, and click on the create mapping icon as shown.

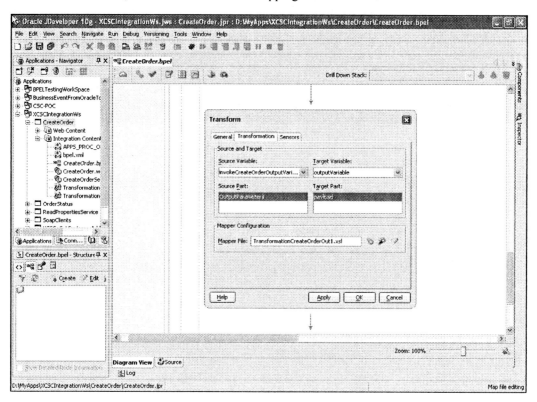

Map the source and target schemas, as shown in the following screenshot:

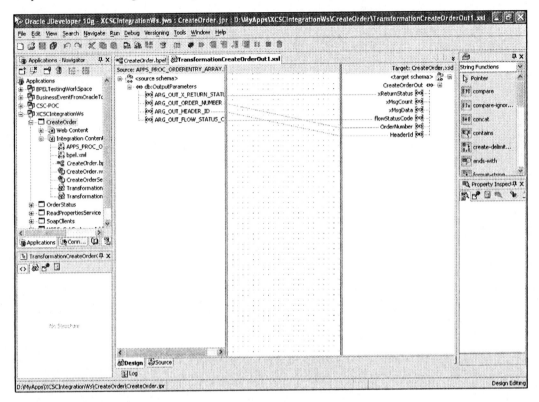

The following files, all available in the sample code download, will recreate the process described in BPEL Designer.

Bpel.xml	The deployment descriptor file that defines the locations of the WSDL files for services to be called by this BPEL process flow.
CreateOrder.xsd	The schema for the input XML submitted by the PeopleSoft application.
CreateOrder.bpel	The process source file containing process flow, partner links, data variables, and necessary fault handlers.
CreateOrder.wsdl	The WSDL client interface, which defines the input and output messages for this BPEL process flow, the supported client interface and operations, and other features. This functionality enables the BPEL process flow to be called as a service.

You have now completed the design of the BPEL process. Next, we'll take a detailed look at configuring the OA Adapter, followed by the configuration at the PeopleSoft end.

Step 2: Configure OA Adapter

OA Adapter is deployed in Oracle Containers for J2EE in managed mode. It can be used to send and receive messages from E-Business Suite. Here are the steps involved in configuring the adapter:

1. Define an Adapter Service and select Oracle Applications adapter.

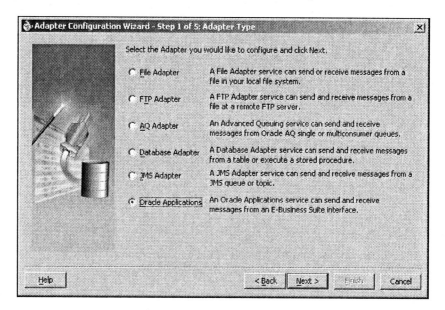

2. Enter a service name. This name will be used as the web service for the selected API/table.

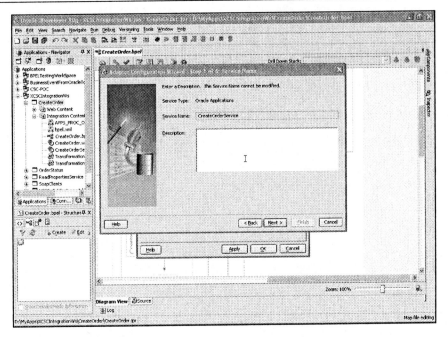

3. Select a database connection that is defined in the project. If there is no database connection available, click on New and follow the wizard.

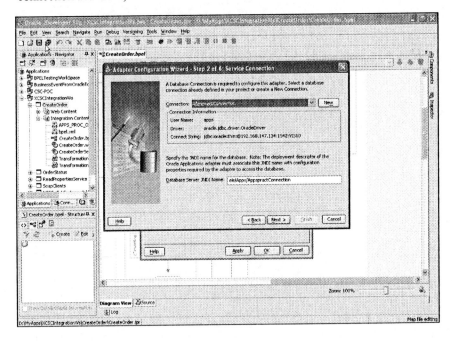

4. Select the Table/Views/APIs interface to the Oracle Application Data.

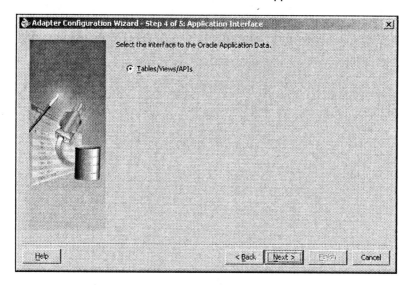

5. Search for and select the PROC_ORDERENTRY_ARRAY API that is to be invoked from the BPEL process.

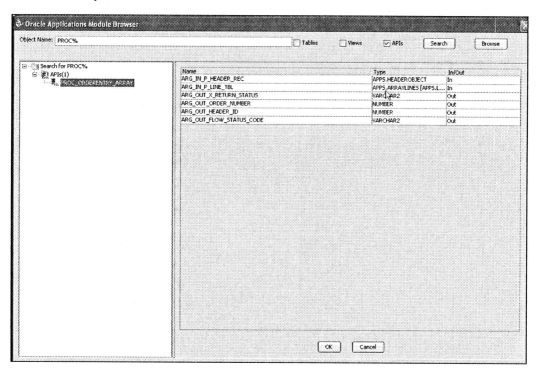

In this case, PROC_ORDERENTRY_ARRAY is the wrapper API written for the PROCESS_ORDER pre-seeded API because BPEL Process Manager will not support the oracle record type. Instead, you will use object types in a wrapper procedure similar to the record types used in PROCESS_ORDER. This interface is responsible for processing the sales order in Oracle Apps.

6. The API will be added to the Adapter Service.

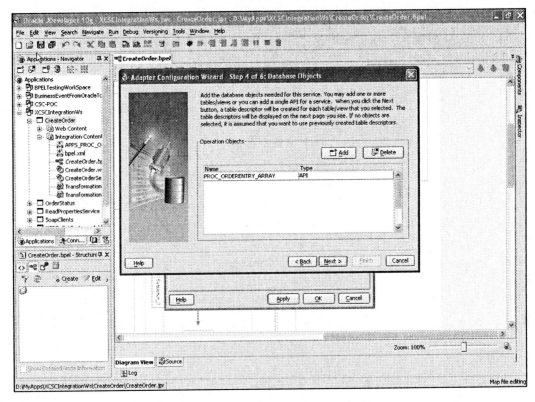

7. The Oracle Applications partner link will be added to the BPEL process, and APPS_PROC_ORDERENTRY_ARRAY.xsd will be created.

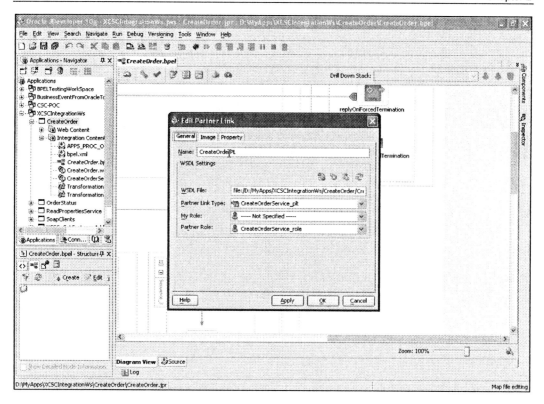

A WSDL file will be created by the Adapter Service for the PROC_ORDERENTERY_ARRAY API, which behaves like a web service and binds to the ERP using WSIF.

The following files in the sample code download will help you configure the OA Adapter in BPEL Designer:

Proc_orderentry_array.sql	Custom wrapper API to invoke OA seeded Process_Order API.
Create_ObjectScript.sql	Contains the "Creation of Objects" script used in the PROC_ORDERENTERY_ARRAY custom API.
CreateOrder.bpel	The process source file containing process flow, partner links, data variables, and necessary fault handlers.
CreateOrder.wsdl	The WSDL client interface, which defines the input and output messages for this BPEL process flow, the supported client interface and operations, and other features. This functionality enables the BPEL process flow to be called as a service.

This completes the design of the BPEL process and the configuration of OA Adapter. Next (and finally), we'll configure PeopleSoft.

Step 3: Configure PeopleSoft

Now that you have created the BPEL process, let's look at the four-step process in configuring PeopleSoft.

- In Step 1, import the BPEL process WSDL into PeopleSoft. You will then use the imported WSDL to configure a node. This node will eventually communicate with the BPEL process.

- In Step 2, configure the Sales Order EIP to invoke this node whenever a new sales order is created.

- Finally, before the node sends the order information to BPEL process, you would need to transform it into a SOAP XML. Hence, in Step 3 and 4, you will write a small PeopleCode function to perform this transformation and establish its relationship with the node.

Let's drill down into each of these steps.

Configure the PeopleSoft Node to Interact with the BPEL Process

In this step, we will configure a node to interact with the BPEL process. We will define the request and response messages and channels on which these messages will travel.

First, import `CreateOrder.wsdl` (created previously) into PeopleSoft using the URL option. This identifies CreateOrder as the process, that will be invoked when an order is created in PeopleSoft. Upon importing the WSDL into PeopleSoft, the Integration Broker adds it to the WSDL repository.

To import `CreateOrder.wsdl`, select PeopleTools | Integration Broker | Web Services | Import WSDL.

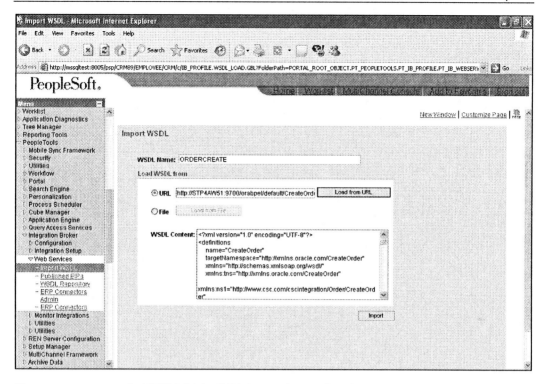

You can now access the WSDL in the WSDL repository using the WSDL Repository page.

Once the CreateOrder WSDL is imported into PeopleSoft, a remote node has to be configured to communicate with the BPEL process. To define this communication, you have to add the corresponding *request message*, *response message*, and *message channel*.

To create a new remote node:

1. Select the Create a New Node Definition option.

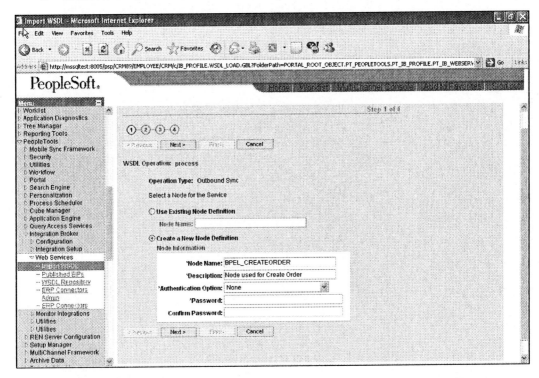

2. In the Node Name field, enter BPEL_CREATEORDER for the new node definition.
3. In the Description field, enter a descriptive name for the node.
4. From the Authentication Option drop-down list, select an authentication method. The valid options are None (the default), Certificate, or Password.
5. In the (optional) Password field, enter a password.
6. In the (optional) Confirm Password field, re-enter the password.

Click on the Next button to proceed to the next page in the WSDL Operation Wizard, where you select request and response messages for the service. Request and response messages are unstructured messages that you create in PeopleSoft to represent SOAP Request and Response messages.

To create a new request or response message:

1. Select the Create a New Message option in the appropriate section.
2. To create a new request message, select the option in the Request Message section. Enter BPEL_ORDER_REQ in the Message Name field.

3. To create a new response message, select the option in the Response Message section. Enter BPEL_ORDER_RES in the Message Name field.

4. Newly created messages default the message version to VERSION_1. PeopleSoft Integration Broker populates the Message Version field with this value.

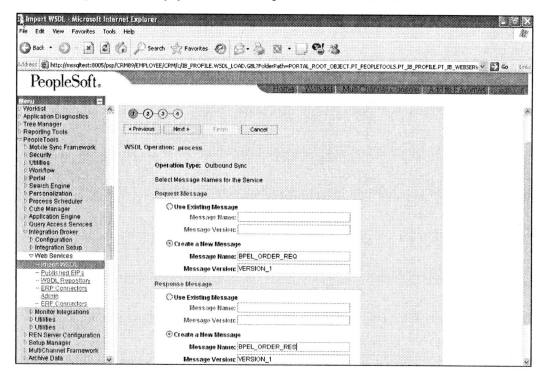

PeopleSoft Integration Broker automatically assigns the new message to the new message channel. At the end of the wizard configuration, the outbound synchronous transaction is created on the node using the new messages.

5. Enter the new message channel name in the Channel Name field as BPEL_SERVICES.

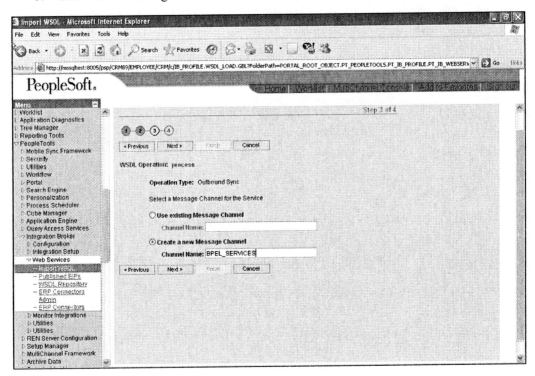

This completes Step 1 of configuring PeopleSoft. You imported the WSDL to tell PeopleSoft which web service to call. You also defined node, messages, and channels to pass information to the web service (BPEL process CreateOrder). In the next step, you will establish a relationship between the Sales order EIP and this newly configured node.

Establish Relationship between EIP and Node

This step will create a link between the CRM_SALES_ORDER EIP and the new node. When the CRM_SALES_ORDER EIP is published to the Integration Broker, the link that we just created will send the CRM_SALES_ORDER message to the remote node we just created, as a request message.

1. Select Node Definition from the People Tools | Integration Setup; search for the BPEL_CREATEORDER node.

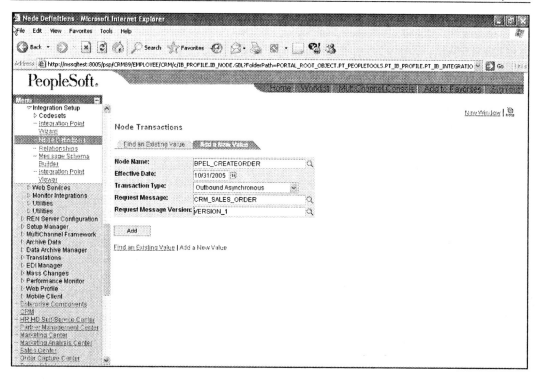

2. In this selected node, change the Transaction Type to Outbound Asynchronous, and enter CRM_SALES_ORDER as Request Message.

Create Transformation Code

In this step, you will create the Application Engine program WSDL_ORDER. (Application Engine is the PeopleSoft high-volume application processor. Application Engine programs are developed with the Application Designer and can leverage common PeopleTools objects such as records, PeopleCode, and SQL objects.) WSDL_ORDER will transform the sales order message received from the EIP to a BPEL request (SOAP message) and publish the transformed message on the node channel.

Add the following code to transform and send the request to the node we created earlier. Once the request is submitted to the node, the node will invoke the web service configured to it. The web service will be invoked and the response is sent back to the node, which sends the XML message to the PeopleCode method.

```
/* Get the data from the AE Runtime */
Local TransformData &transformData = %TransformData;

Local File &logFile = GetFile("TestSyncReqResStep3.log", "W",
%FilePath_Absolute);

Local string &destNode = &transformData.DestNode;

&logFile.WriteLine("DestNode: " | &destNode);

/* Set a temp object to contain the incoming document */
Local XmlDoc &xmlDoc = &transformData.XmlDoc;
```

```
Local string &xmlStr = &xmlDoc.GenXmlString();

&logFile.WriteLine("Transformed XML : " | &xmlStr);

/* Maps the &xmlDoc  to the BPEL_ORDER_REQ and
   publish to the BPEL_CREATEORDER node.
   Node will invoke BPEL CreateOrder process.
   Response will be assigned to &response variable. */

Local XmlDoc &response = SyncRequestXmlDoc(&xmlDoc, Message.BPEL_ORDER_REQ,
Node.BPEL_CREATEORDER);

&logFile.WriteLine("Response XML Data: " | &response.GenXmlString());

&logFile.Close();
```

Linking WSDL_ORDER Apps Engine Program with the Node

In this step, you will relate the transformation code to the CreateOrder node. Hence, whenever BPEL Process Manager is invoked, this transformation code will be executed.

Create a new relationship WSDL_ORDER and map it to the WSDL_ORDER node. To do that:

Select Relationships from the People Tools | Integration Setup and select Add New Value.

1. Map the initial node as BPEL_CREATEORDER, Request Message Name as CRM_SALES_ORDER , Transaction Type as OA , Result Node as BPEL_CREATEORDER, and Request Message Name as CRM_SALES_ORDER and their versions will be selected by default. Then click on Add.

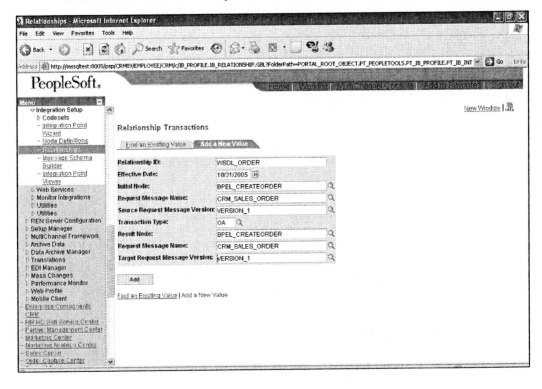

2. Map the transformation Request as WSDL_ORDER.

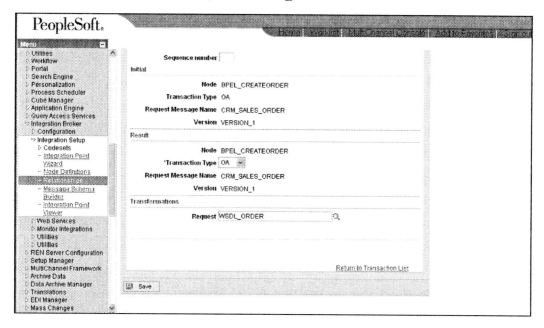

This completes the sales order creation steps. Again, watch the design time-viewlet (`http://www.oracle.com/technology/pub/articles/bpel_cookbook/files/ configuration_setup_viewlet_version3.0_viewlet.html`) to see how all these steps are configured; in the run-time viewlet (`http://www.oracle.com/technology/pub/articles/ bpel_cookbook/files/psft_bpel_oracle_ordercreation_2.0.html`), you will actually see a sales order being submitted from PeopleSoft and traveling to Oracle Apps.

Conclusion

With heterogeneous applications across multiple different business units, organizations have challenges aggregating information. Integrating these systems represents a huge investment. Now, as demonstrated here, such organizations have a choice to easily integrate such applications using standards like BPEL.

3

Building the Service Value Chain

by Yves Coene and The Hoa Nguyen

A case study in how the European Space Agency used BPEL scopes, BPEL domains, and the Oracle BPEL Process Manager API to build a partner-friendly web services network.

Buoyed by maturing web service standards, more and more organizations are using web services in a collaborative environment. BPEL is fast becoming the platform for orchestrating these web services for inter-enterprise collaboration. BPEL offers the compelling benefits of a standards-based approach and loosely-coupled process integration to companies building an online marketplace or collaborative network.

Yet the exciting new capabilities offered by web services carry some risk. In many cases, partner relationships break down or integration costs skyrocket if certain technical and administrative challenges are not addressed at design time:

- Partners must agree well in advance to conduct business according to specific criteria. Transport protocol, purpose of the interaction, message format, and business constraints have to be communicated clearly.

- Joining the network has to be an easy process; collaborative networks become successful mainly through growth.

- Users must easily find business services at run time, or the promise of services-oriented architecture (SOA) is largely lost. (Service repositories are useful for this purpose.) If developers cannot readily find and reuse services, the services essentially don't exist.

- Partners should have the ability to monitor web services in real time. End users should be able to track the progress of a specific order, and trading partners diagnose a specific bottleneck within a business process.

These challenges are intensified when a collaborative network operates in a hosted environment. In that model, partners expose the functionality provided by their legacy applications as a web service. This web service is published into a centralized repository. The host is responsible for orchestrating the complex business processes, which in turn, leverage partner web services.

In this chapter of *The BPEL Cookbook*, I will explain the architectural considerations associated with these challenges, using a European Space Agency (ESA) project on which our team from SpaceBel SA was involved, as a case study. We will also discuss how this project leveraged BPEL scopes, BPEL domains, and the Oracle BPEL Process Manager API to build a "partner-friendly" collaborative network.

Overview of the ESA Network

The ESA has embarked on a strategic initiative to create a BPEL-driven collaborative network of service providers based entirely on open standards. This network, referred to as the **Service Support Environment (SSE)** network, combines **Earth Observation (EO)** and **Geographic Information System (GIS)** services from third parties to provide value-added composite services. SSE is a growing network currently including more than 20 partners spread across nine different countries.

As shown in the figure below, SSE is a simple realization of a BPEL-enabled network. ESA acts as an intermediary broker that supports process-based collaboration between different partners on web services standards such as SOAP, WSDL, WS-Addressing, and WS-Inspection, among others. This network operates in a hub-and-spoke topology: Service providers use Oracle BPEL Designer to contribute different types of Earth Observation and GIS services into a centralized repository, thereby creating an ever-expanding catalog of services.

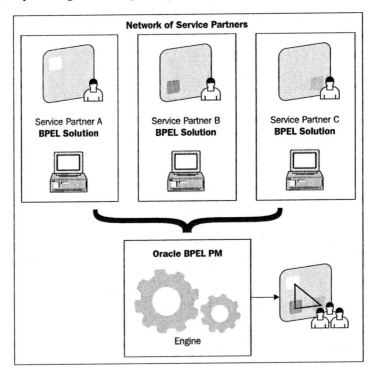

SSE provides the necessary infrastructure to:

- Host and manage the central repository that serves as a catalog of available services
- Register and search services inside the central directory
- Execute short-lived and long-lived business processes inside the Oracle BPEL engine
- Enable partners to monitor the execution of web services using the Oracle BPEL Process Manager console

End users request specific services by browsing the catalog of available services. Upon request, SSE invokes the associated business process. This business process calls the web service (which runs at the service provider's location) to complete the request.

SSE allows synchronous as well as asynchronous models of interaction. ESA has leveraged the Oracle BPEL Process Manager API extensively to offer the utmost flexibility and ease of use to service providers and end users.

Designing a Web Services Network

Open standards are changing the rules of integration. BPEL offers a process-centric approach to cross-enterprise integration, whereby partner interactions are defined using BPEL process flows. This blend of SOA with BPEL provides a unique opportunity to build a loosely coupled collaborative network.

Hub and spoke (the approach taken with SSE) is the widely used network topology wherein one organization establishes a connection with various partners. Alternatively, the network can adopt a unilateral peer-to-peer model. In this case, every partner provides a platform for web services security and provisioning.

Now, let's examine the four areas of network design:

- Setting up the interface relationship
- Simplifying partner enablement
- Creating a centralized service registry
- Empowering partners and end users with self-service monitoring

Setting Up the Interface Relationship

Collaborative network design begins with defining the rules of engagement. These rules specify the messages exchanged within a business process, the sequence in which these messages are exchanged, and the physical attributes of the messages. In order to communicate properly, all partners have to be able to answer the following questions:

- **Purpose of the interaction**: Is this request for a quote or purchase order?
- **Message format**: How is the message encoded?
- **Vocabulary**: How should our messages be structured so that other parties can understand and process them?

- **Business constraints**: How soon should we respond to a request?
- **Communication channel**: Should our messages be encrypted?

To help partners get those answers, ESA publicly published an *Interface Control Document* (http://services.eoportal.org/massRef/documentation/icd.pdf) to define these terms. This document formalizes the technical integration rules that were established, refined, and validated during several ESA-funded projects. Message-based SOAP over HTTP or HTTPS for secure communication are the protocols for communication between the SSE server and service providers. (As of this writing, we are analyzing the use of WS-Security.) **Web Services Definition Language (WSDL)** is the only interface contract binding all entities; the service provider has to create a WSDL file that describes its SOAP interface and makes it available for other partners. Some of the information contained in the WSDL file is fixed, but the following information has to be provided:

- Selected operations according to the selected interaction model (search, RFQ, order)
- Physical location of the services
- Import of service XSD Schema

To facilitate comparison of services, consistency, and message translations, ESA mandates the use of XSD Schema to express the XML payloads. SSE also requires the use of a master XSLT document to ensure consistency in the presentation layer. The template stylesheet has to be imported in each service as follows:

```
<xsl:stylesheet version="1.0"
    xmlns:xsl="http://www.w3.org/1999/XSL/Transform"
    xmlns:oi="http://www.esa.int/oi">
<!-- Import statements -->
<xsl:import href="./SSE.xsl"/>
<!-- Apply the template for the root element from SSE standard template -->
<xsl:template match="/">
<xsl:apply-imports/>
</xsl:template>
...
```

xsl:apply-imports processes the root node using the template rules imported from the SSE stylesheet. When registering the service, the service provider provides the URL of the XML Schema, WSDL, and XSLT file. The SSE imposes the use of document-style SOAP. This approach allows for detailed specification of service input and output data, as well as validation of incoming and outgoing messages using XML Schema.

The approach adopted by ESA offers a quick-turnaround solution for companies looking to start a web-services network with a limited number of partners. As the network size grows, new variants of message formats, communication rules, security, and transport mechanisms will need to be introduced.

Simplifying Partner Enablement

The growth of any network relies on the ease with which new partners can join and participate. The following factors will have a large impact on this process:

- **Integration with hub**: How do partners create and submit their web services? Can the hub support different transport protocols?

- **Process management**: Is there a proper delineation between different partner processes? Can a partner modify its business process without affecting the reliability of the entire network? Can processes be generated on the fly using metadata definition?

SSE has been successful in forging stronger ties with its partners by simplifying the technical demands placed on service providers. ESA accomplishes this goal by distributing partner connectivity software, partitioning the development platform, and automatically generating process flows on behalf of the partners.

For example, to speed up the integration process, ESA distributes SSE Toolbox, a free toolkit that acts as an interface between SSE and service providers' existing systems. SSE Toolbox, which is based on the Sun Java Web Services Developer Pack, provides an XML scripting language supporting various back-end integration mechanisms such as HTTP, FTP, file exchange, JDBC, calling a Java API, and so on. It also automatically generates the WSDL file that is required to register the service.

Different partners contribute multiple services into the central repository. Partitioning the development and deployment environment shields partners from each other's changes. SSE effectively leverages partitioning by using BPEL domains within the Oracle BPEL Process Manager. BPEL domains allow a developer or administrator to partition a single instance of the Oracle BPEL Process Manager into multiple virtual BPEL **sandboxes**. A BPEL domain is identified by an ID and protected with a password. When a service provider registers on SSE, the Oracle BPEL Process Manager API is invoked to automatically create a BPEL domain to hold service definition files.

Here's an example of a `createDomain()` method:

```
/**
 * Create new domain space for a service provider to
 * hold her/his services workflow definitions files in
 *
 * @param domainName The Id to identify the domain
 * @param password The password used to login to the corresponding domain
 * @exception RemoteException System communication error
 * @exception WorkflowException Thrown if any error happens on the server
 *      that prevent the delete
 *
 */
public void createDomain(String domainName, String password)
    throws RemoteException, WorkflowException{
  if(ml.isDebugEnabled()) ml.debug("Enter createDomain(domain = " +
                          domainName + " password = " + password);
  /**
   * check if the being created domain exist?
   */

  try {
    Locator locator = new Locator(domainName, password);
    ml.info("Stop creating domain: " + domainName +
        " because it has already existed.");
    throw new WorkflowException("1019");
```

```
            } catch (com.oracle.bpel.client.ServerException e) {
                ;
            }
            try {
                //obtain the domain admin password from the system configuration
                // SSE.properties file
                String domainAdminPassword = SystemConfigurationInfo.getProperty
                    (WorkflowConstant.BPEL_DOMAIN_ADMIN_PASSWORD);
                ServerAuth auth = ServerAuthFactory.authenticate(
                                domainAdminPassword, "localhost" );
                if(ml.isDebugEnabled()) ml.debug("obtain authentication ok");
                // Create server object ... this is our service interface
                //
                Server server = new Server( auth );
                // Domain id is "newDomain", the password is "myPassword"
                if(ml.isDebugEnabled()) ml.debug("create server instance ok");
                //
                  Map domainProperties = new HashMap();
                  domainProperties.put( Configuration.DATASOURCE_JNDI,
                                SystemConfigurationInfo.getProperty
                  (CommonConstant.DEFAULT_BPELDOMAIN_DS_JNDI));
                  domainProperties.put( Configuration.TX_DATASOURCE_JNDI,
                                SystemConfigurationInfo.getProperty
                  (CommonConstant.DEFAULT_BPELDOMAIN_DS_JNDI));

                if(ml.isDebugEnabled()) ml.debug(
                            "create domain - ds jndi property key/value: " +
                            Configuration.DATASOURCE_JNDI + "/" +
                            SystemConfigurationInfo.getProperty(
                                CommonConstant.DEFAULT_BPELDOMAIN_DS_JNDI));
                if(ml.isDebugEnabled()) ml.debug(
                            "create domain - tx_ds jndi property key/value: " +
                            Configuration.TX_DATASOURCE_JNDI + "/" +
                            SystemConfigurationInfo.getProperty(
                                CommonConstant.DEFAULT_BPELDOMAIN_DS_JNDI));
            server.createDomain(domainName, password, domainProperties);

                if(ml.isDebugEnabled()) ml.debug("Enter createDomain
                    (domain = " + domainName + " password = " + password);

        } catch( com.oracle.bpel.client.ServerException se ){
            ml.error(se.getMessage());
            if(ml.isDebugEnabled()) se.printStackTrace();
            throw new WorkflowException("1018", se.getCause());
        }
    }
}
```

In the implementation of the runBuildScript method that follows, the Oracle bpelc function is accessed via an Ant build script. The runBuildScript method invokes an Ant project file that in turn invokes bpelc to compile and deploy the service provider's BPEL process.

```
/**
 * execute the ant script to build an Oracle BPEL process
 * that implements the workflow.
 * The script also deploys the workflow to the service domains.
 * All input information is provided under the props at the input param.
 * @param props Contain all necessary properties used to build/deploy
        the workflow BPEL process
 * @throws WorkflowException
 */
private void runBuildScript(String buildFilename, Properties props)
    throws WorkflowException{
        if(ml.isDebugEnabled())ml.debug("Enter runBuildScript(buildFileName = "
```

```
                    + buildFilename +
                    ", properties = ...");
             try {
                Project project = new Project();
                project.init();
                File buildFile = new File(buildFilename);

                if (!buildFile.exists()) throw new WorkflowException("1015");
                if(ml.isDebugEnabled()) ml.debug("ant build file: " +
                                                  buildFile.getAbsolutePath());

                ProjectHelper.configureProject(project, buildFile);
                //prepare logger for the project build
                PrintStream out = System.out;
                BuildLogger logger = new DefaultLogger();
                logger.setMessageOutputLevel(Project.MSG_DEBUG);
                logger.setOutputPrintStream(out);
                logger.setErrorPrintStream(out);
                project.addBuildListener(logger);

                //set project properties
                Enumeration keys = props.keys();
                while(keys.hasMoreElements()){
                   String key = keys.nextElement().toString();
                   project.setProperty(key, props.getProperty(key));
                }
                // test
                //excute default target
                project.executeTarget(project.getDefaultTarget());
                   if(ml.isDebugEnabled())ml.debug("Exit runBuildScript
                            (buildFileName = " + buildFilename +
                                ", properties = ...");
             }
             catch (Exception ex) {
                ml.error(ex.getMessage());
                if(ml.isDebugEnabled()) ex.printStackTrace();
                throw new WorkflowException("1002",ex.getCause());
             }
        }
```

In your web services network design, you should consider using BPEL domains to segregate the process design and deployment platform for all involved parties. Here are some possible applications:

- Partition a single Oracle BPEL Process Manager instance into a multi-developer environment. In this case the domain ID usually identifies the developer owning that domain.

- Partition a single Oracle BPEL Process Manager instance into development and QA environments. In that case the domain IDs might be "test" and "QA".

- Partition a single Oracle BPEL Process Manager instance into an environment that can be used by multiple departments or partners. In these cases, the domain IDs are the names of the departments or partners.

Creating a Central Service Registry

After you have defined the network relationships, partners are free to join and contribute their services. The ability to publish and search these services, of course, is one of the underpinnings of an SOA platform.

In this process, partners publish their web services to a central registry where all information about the service is managed. This central framework promotes service reusability and minimizes the effort and time required to locate a service. The lack of a central registry degrades the flexibility and openness of a network, leading to inconsistency and chaos.

The SSE network leverages a central web-services repository heavily; partners use **Web Services Inspection Language (WSIL)** for discovery of available services. Service providers have the ability to reuse existing web services (offered by other providers within the network) by selecting the respective WSDL files. This task is accomplished by adding the WS-Inspection URL `http://services.eoportal.org/inspection.wsil` in the Oracle BPEL Designer tool configuration file `UDDIProviderList.xml`, as shown here:

```
<provider>
    <description>ESA SSE Portal</description>
    <type>wsil</type>
    <inquiryURL>
        http://services.eoportal.org/inspection.wsil
    </inquiryURL>
</provider>
```

The Oracle BPEL Designer at the service provider location connects to the SSE server and discovers the available services and their WSDL files using the WS-Inspection protocol. After connecting to the WS-Inspection server, the list of all available services is displayed, as shown in the screenshot below:

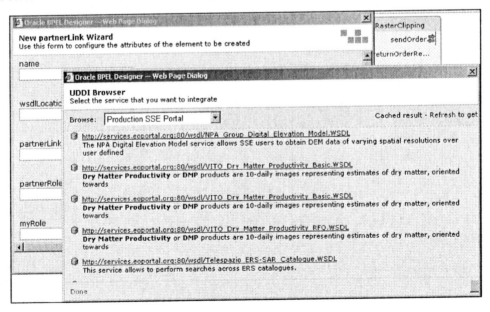

For each service, a corresponding WSDL file and short textual description is provided. A partner link for this service is added by selecting the WSDL file. When the process flow has been built, it is deployed on the SSE portal using the BPEL console. (In its next release, SSE will integrate UDDI registry with Oracle BPEL. When a new service is registered, it will automatically be registered in this UDDI registry as well. This integration will facilitate service discovery by external tools, which now is only possible if these tools support WS-Inspection.)

Although you can build SOA and achieve many of its benefits without establishing a service repository, a repository is indispensable in the long term. Architecture can cope without a repository if the scope of the service is just one project. However, most enterprise scenarios are characterized by variety of services and partners, with most of them being in constant flux.

Providing Self-Service Monitoring

In a collaborative network where multiple parties participate in a business process, monitoring the execution of a business process is crucial so that key performance indicators around business processes can be tied to service-level agreements. (For example, one of the key requirements to join the network could be to acknowledge the request for a quote within two hours.) Monitoring of business processes can offer key insight into how long a specific business process instance takes to execute, why delays occur, and how the problem could be rectified for future transactions.

This level of diagnosis should be offered to the partners and the end users. By creating a self-service environment, partners and end users have the ability to track their individual processes and, in turn, alleviate the problems detected by a centralized monitoring framework.

The Oracle BPEL Console can be used to monitor and debug business processes (see the figure overleaf). ESA and service providers leverage the BPEL Console to track how many BPEL process instances are running and completed, the average duration of a process instance (to get detailed breakdown of time consumption within the process), and the process instance audit trail in text format, allowing partners to view intermediate results.

In addition, end users ordering a specific service have the ability to track the state of their order. This information is presented outside the BPEL Console using the Oracle BPEL Process Manager API. Service providers are encouraged to use meaningful scope names in their BPEL processes; at run time, the portal extracts the name of the current BPEL "scope" using the IInstanceHandle.getStatus() API to present this progress information to the end user.

Scopes are hierarchically organized parts into which a complex business process can be divided. They provide behavioral contexts for activities. By using meaningful scope names in BPEL process, it is possible for partners to track the status of "short-lived" and "long-lived" business processes.

For example, see the implementation of the getOrderSubstatus method below. This method allows ESS partners to get the current status of the BPEL process instance using the name of the scope being executed in the BPEL file.

```
/* call the Oracle BPEL API to get current status of the workflow instance,
 * corresponding to the ordered supplied at the input
 * @param ordered The order identified
 * @param workflowId The workflow name (or ID) that is processing the order
 * stage.
```

```
 * Normally, there are two stages of an order:
 *     send(process)rfq and send(process) order
 * @param domain The domain that the order workflow belongs to
 * @param password The password used to login to the workflow domain
 * @return the current status of the workflow instance - particularly,
 * it is the name of the current active scope in the workflow BPEL file.
 * @throws RemoteException
 * @throws WorkflowException
 */
public String getOrderSubstatus(String ordered, String workflowId,
                                String domain, String password)
  throws RemoteException, WorkflowException
{
    if(ml.isDebugEnabled()) ml.debug("Enter getOrderSubstatus(ordered = " +
                ordered + ", workflowId = " + workflowId + ", domain = " +
                domain + ", password = " + password);
    String status = "";
    try {

        Locator locator = new Locator(domain, password);
        IinstanceHandle instance = locator.lookupInstance(ordered + "_" +
                                                          workflowId);

        if( instance.isComplete() )  status = "Completed";
        else status = instance.getStatus();

        return status;
    } catch (com.oracle.bpel.client.ServerException e) {
        // TODO Auto-generated catch block

        ml.error(e.getMessage());
        if(ml.isDebugEnabled()) e.printStackTrace();
        throw new WorkflowException("1016", e.getCause());
    }

}
```

Conclusion

The ESA has built its entire collaborative network with agility in mind. Interface relationships have been flexibly defined to facilitate easier adoption and rapid evolution. Its use of BPEL domains to offer an independent workspace offers massive flexibility to service providers; providers can modify their business processes without affecting the stability of the network. BPEL scopes have enabled ESA to track the status of the in-flight processes at the micro level. BPEL process flows are generated automatically on behalf of service providers. All these factors cumulatively contribute towards making the network more partner-friendly, and minimize the upfront investment by the partner.

However, there are other areas of network design—such as distributed transaction management, security, and trading partner management—that we have not addressed here. As B2B networks grow in size, BPEL can take the lead in orchestrating private processes. For example, the Oracle Integration B2B product, which is interoperable with Oracle BPEL Process Manager, addresses public process choreography, handshake protocol support (RosettaNet, ebXML, EDI, and HIPAA), message formats handling (MIME, SMIME, AS2, and XMLDSig), and trading partner management (non-repudiation, service-level agreements, and partner agreements).

4

A Services-Oriented Approach to Business Rules Development

by Kevin Geminiuc

Learn how to reduce maintenance costs and improve organizational flexibility through a services-oriented approach to business rules development and management.

Many organizations are moving from an object-oriented paradigm for managing business processes toward a service-oriented approach; indeed, services are becoming the fundamental elements of application development. At the same time, Business Process Execution Language (BPEL) has become the de facto standard for orchestrating these services and managing flawless execution of business process. The confluence of these trends is presenting some interesting opportunities for more flexible, cost-effective management of business processes.

Most business processes—loan-approval processes being a good example—contain multiple decision points. At these decision points, certain criteria are evaluated. Based on these criteria or **business rules**, business processes change their behavior. In essence, these business rules drive the business process. Frequently, these rules are embedded within the business process itself or inside custom Java code, which can cause several problems down the road:

- Business rules change more often than the processes themselves, but changing and managing embedded business rules is a complex task beyond the abilities of most business analysts. Thus, as business rules change, programmers often have to commit expensive time to this task.

- Most organizations lack a central rules repository. Consequently, any organization-wide change in policy cannot be applied across all business processes.

- Business processes cannot reuse rules. Hence, IT personnel end up designing rules for each and every process, often leading to inconsistency or redundancy.

The best way to avoid these problems is to use a **rules engine** to separate business processes from business rules. In this approach, rules are exposed as services and BPEL processes leverage these services by querying the engine when they reach decision points. This approach is much more flexible—instead of coding rules in programming languages or inside a process, rules can be manipulated graphically. Business users with tools can write rules themselves, and can make post-deployment rule changes without IT assistance. With business users doing most of the updates and enhancements, maintenance costs can reduce substantially.

Rules engines and BPEL are complementary technologies. Oracle BPEL Process Manager provides high-level tools to visualize, design, and manage BPEL process flows, whereas third-party rules engines allow complicated business logic to be expressed in English-like syntax and edited by nonprogrammer domain experts.

In this chapter of *The BPEL Cookbook*, I'll provide best practices for separation of process and rules based on my team's own experience. Using code examples, I'll also offer a development approach and change-management strategy for integrating BPEL with a rules engine. Finally, I'll explain how this architecture leads to proper separation of logic across different layers.

Separating Rules from Processes

Integrating a rules engine within a process-management framework requires some investment up front. Before you attempt this integration, it is important to delineate rules from process. Hence, a major decision in system architecture is how to implement business policies, business processes, and supporting business logic. Indeed, the architect must communicate or invent best practices so that designers know where each of the relevant technologies—BPEL, business rules, Java/web services—should be applied when designing system functionality.

As illustrated in the figure below, business logic is spread across three different layers of the IT infrastructure: business process, web services, and rules. Let's address each in turn.

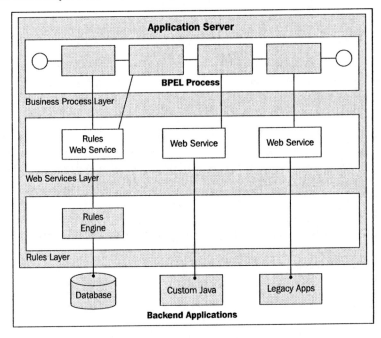

Business Process Layer

This layer is responsible for managing the overall execution of the business process. These business processes, implemented using BPEL, can be long running, transactional, and persistent. Process logic supports high-level transactions ("sagas") across web-service/EJB calls as well as nested sub-process transactions. The BPEL engine supports audit and instrumentation of workflow and thus is well suited for:

- Separating less volatile workflow steps from more volatile business rules
- Implementing line-of-business processes
- Implementing process flows requiring compensation
- Supporting large-scale instantiation of process flows
- Designing process flows that need auditing
- Orchestrating heterogeneous technologies such as connectors, web services, and Web Services Invocation Framework (WSIF)-enabled logic

Web Service Layer

The web services layer exposes the existing application layer functionality as services. Multiple business processes can then reuse these services, thereby fulfilling the promise of a **service-oriented architecture (SOA)**.

Web services implement functional and domain logic. Functional methods are typically stateless and medium-grained. Web services may, for example, contain utility methods, entity operations, and inquiry methods for system data. You can implement web services using multiple technologies and hide differences among implementation platforms. Thus, this layer is well suited for:

- Implementing medium-grained methods for a particular entity/domain area
- Integrating legacy code/third-party tools
- Encapsulating logic, custom code, and implementation from the application layer

Rules Layer

The rules engine is typically the home for complex logic that involves a number of interdependencies between entities and order-dependent logic calculation. Extracting business rules as a separate entity from business process leads to better decoupling of the system, which, in consequence, increases maintainability.

Rules engines allow for evaluation of rules sets in parallel and in a sequential order. In addition, rules engines have the ability to evaluate the values of input and intermediate data and determine if a rule should be fired. This modular design provides a simpler and more maintainable solution than traditional Java procedural code.

Furthermore, as I mentioned previously, rules are declarative and allow high-level GUI editing by business analysts. Modern rules engines execute extremely quickly and provide built-in audit logging. The typical traits of a rules layer are:

- Contains coupled and complex logic
- Supports efficient business logic evaluation using parallel execution
- Contains complex return structures built from multiple business rule evaluations
- Allows for translation of domain logic into simple rules
- Implements highly volatile business policy

Because rules are exposed as services in the web services layer, they can be reused across all inter-enterprise applications, making the development of new applications and integrations easier.

Development and Maintenance

To illustrate the development process, we will use the example of a business process called the Eligibility Process. This process assesses the eligibility of a family for a specific healthcare program. Depending on the attributes of the family (income, total number of children), it assigns the family to Healthcare Program 1 or Healthcare Program 2. During the analysis phase, logic is categorized into different buckets based on volatility and complexity. As discussed in the previous section, rules typically model complex return structures that require multiple business validations as well as policies that change frequently or that influence large parts of the organization. In contrast, departmental or organizational processes are modeled in the business process layer.

The typical development process comprises three steps:

1. Create rules in a ruleset.
2. Expose the ruleset as a web service.
3. Invoke the ruleset web service from BPEL.

The development phase requires specialized roles such as rules developer, process-flow developer, business analyst, and web services developer to accomplish these tasks (see figure opposite).

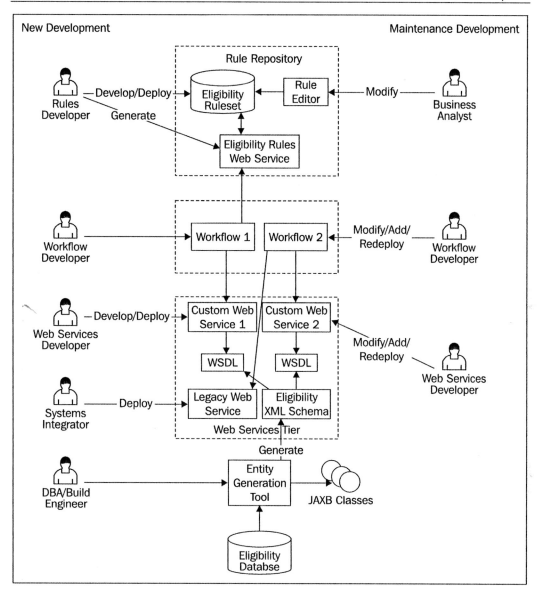

Create Rules in a Ruleset

The development phase begins with a rule developer creating the initial rules in an integrated graphical development environment, such as ILOG's JRules business rule management system. (See the information box for more on business rules functionality in Oracle Fusion Middleware.)

The Oracle Fusion Middleware Rules Engine

This example illustrates the integration of ILOG's rules engine with Oracle BPEL Process Manager, but note that a future release of Oracle Fusion Middleware will integrate a new, native business rules engine with Oracle BPEL Process Manager.

A Decision Service wizard in Oracle BPEL Designer will allow users to incorporate business rules into a BPEL project. It will include the ability to browse repositories of Oracle Business Rules as well as third-party rules engines. In addition, users will be able to map BPEL variables to facts in the rule repository and assert new facts and execute rules. Then, the BPEL engine will automatically perform any format translation from XML-based variables to the Java-based datatypes for the rules engine facts.

Post deployment, business users will be able to access rules related to the business process and make changes without redeploying the process. This approach will greatly simplify the integration of BPEL processes with rules engines and enhance the agility of the architecture.

Prior to creating a rule, the rule repository and object model need to be set up. The rule repository allows for the maintenance and management of business rules across their lifecycle. The problem domain that business rules manipulate is expressed with ILOG JRules in the form of a business object model (BOM). A BOM is represented via Java classes or an XML schema representing an executable version of the model. XML Schema can help ensure data agility. Detailed implementation of the object model is usually a task for developers.

After developers have created the object model and rule repository, you need to decide which rules will be maintainable by analysts versus which rules are to be developed in the low-level language (IRL). After creating the developer-level rules, the developers work with analysts to identify the remaining rules and capture them in rule templates, which can be reused by multiple non-technical parties. This method simplifies and accelerates rule production and reduces the incidence of human error.

To start the template-based rule-creation process, the analyst connects to the rule repository. When he or she has opened the rule package from the repository, they will have access to its BOM. ILOG supports the definition of high-level rules through its **Business Application Language (BAL)**. The analyst can edit an existing rule or create new rules at this point. Rules may be modified through a template during the maintenance phase, which limits what modifications can be made to the rule.

The rule editor has a default template and allows a developer to create conditions and actions using the IF–THEN construct. As shown in the figure opposite, the business analyst is creating a rule that checks the total number of children in the family. If this variable equals 2, then the family qualifies for Healthcare Program 1. Rule returns the value true in datatype eligibilityResult.

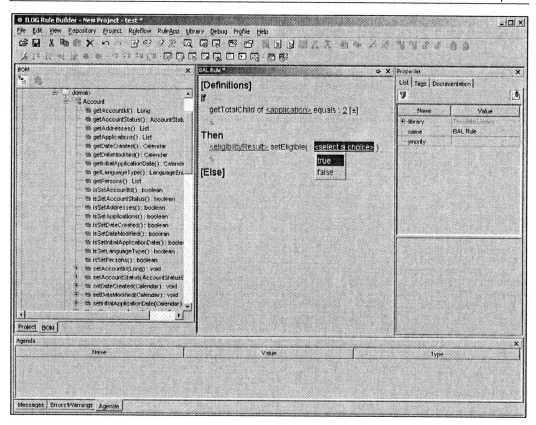

After a new rule is developed, it can be tested with sample data inside the ILOG Rule Builder tool. This debugger in Rule Builder supports breakpoints, allows the user to inspect working memory facts, and displays the rule execution order. When rule editing and testing are complete, the analyst will export the rule package into a ruleset and deploy it back to the repository.

The following code example shows the implementation of the Eligibility ruleset.

```
// Eligibility ruleset receives an account and calculates
// eligibility results for multiple programs

ruleset eligibility {
    in Account account;
    out List eligibilityResultsList = new ArrayList();

}

// calculate program 1 then program 2 eligibility
flowtask Program1_TaskFlow {
    body = {
        Program1_Setup;
        Program1_Eligibility;
        Program2_Setup;
        Program2_Eligibility;
    }
};
```

```
// Determine which rules are setup rules for program 1
ruletask Program1_Setup{
    body = select(?rule) {
        if("Program1_Setup".getTask(?rule) )
            return true;
        else
            return false;
    }
}

// Determine which rules are eligibility rules for program 1
ruletask Program1_Eligibility{
    body = select(?rule) {
        if("Program1_Eligibility".getTask(?rule) )
            return true;
        else
            return false;
    }
}

// Create an eligibility result (JAXB object) for program 1
rule Progam1.CreateEligibilityResult {
    property task = " Program1_Setup";
    when {
        ?account: Account();
        ?person: Person();

    }
    then {
        bind ?result = new EligibilityResult ();
        ?result.setPersonId(?person.getPersonId());
        ?result.setProgramType(ProgramEnum.PROGRAM1);
        ?result.setEligible(Boolean.FALSE);
        modify ?person { getEligibilityResults().add(?result); };
    }
};

// simple rule make person eligible if over 6 years old and returns
// result back in finalResults map
rule Program1.AgeQualification {
    property task = " Program1_Eligibility";
    when {
        ?person: Person(?age: getAge().intValue(););
        evaluate(?age >= 6);
    }
    then {
    modify ?result {setEligible(Boolean.TRUE); };
    finalResults.add(?result);
    }

};
```

Expose the Ruleset as a Web Service

Rules engines such as JRules provide tools to generate wrapper web services or session beans to wrap a newly developed ruleset. Web services developers will be instrumental in creating a wrapper to expose the ruleset as a web service.

XML is a key standard for integrating rules, EJBs, BPEL process flows, and web services. BPEL uses XML natively to access data while web services use it to serialize data (and will use it unmodified in Doc/Literal invocations). XML can be used directly in rules. By marshaling, XML can be transformed directly into a JAXB object tree. Rules can be executed with native Java objects.

Web services should import XML Schema in their respective WSDL definitions. Generated DTO objects from XML Schema (e.g. JAXB) can also help ensure that data is translated smoothly without conversion errors.

The Eligibility web service provides the translation from XML to JAXB and then invokes the Eligibility Rules Delegate session bean. To hide the complexity of invoking JRules custom libraries, you would create a session façade. This approach makes the implementation rules-engine "agnostic"; the system could be easily ported to a new rules engine provider. The Eligibility Rules Delegate session bean makes an RMI call to Eligibility façade session bean. This session bean invokes the Eligibility ruleset in the RuleApp package using
`ruleSession.executeRules("RuleApp/eligibility")`.

```
import ilog.rules.bres.session.IlrRuleExecutionResult;
import ilog.rules.bres.session.IlrStatelessRuleSession;
import ilog.rules.bres.session.ejb.IlrManagedRuleSessionProvider;
import ilog.rules.bres.session.util.IlrRuleSessionHelper;
    .
    .
    .
    public List assessEligibility(AccountRoot account) {

    List eligibilityList = null;
    // get stateless rulesession instance
    IlrStatelessRuleSession ruleSession = null;
    try {
        ruleSession = IlrManagedRuleSessionProvider.getProvider()
                .createStatelessRuleSession();
    } catch (ilog.rules.bres.session.IlrRuleSessionCreationException ce) {
                String msg = "Failed to retrieve RuleSession Provider";
                throw new InfrastructureException(msg, ce);
    }

    // pass borrower and credit as "in" parameters of the stateless session.
    IlrRuleSessionHelper helper = new IlrRuleSessionHelper(false);
    helper.addParameter("account", account);

    try{
    // execute rules and handle results
        IlrRuleExecutionResult res = ruleSession.executeRules(
            "/RuleApp/ eligibility", null,
            helper.getJavaClassResolver(this), helper.getParameters());
        eligibilityList = (List)res.parametersOut.getHandle(
            "finalResults").getValue();
    } catch(Throwable t) {

        String msg = "Failed to execute rule!";
        throw new InfrastructureException(msg, t);
    }
    return eligibilityList;

    }
```

Invoke the Ruleset Web Service from BPEL

After all custom system components are developed, it's time for developers to integrate the system with the BPEL engine. Legacy systems and new custom components are orchestrated by BPEL process flows. Issues with compatibility, datatype conversion, and web service protocols would be addressed at this time. Process-flow developers and/or system integrators would implement the orchestration flows inside Oracle BPEL Process Designer.

For example, BPEL will invoke the underlying Eligibility web service using the following code:

```
<assign name="setAccount">
  <copy>
      <from variable="BPELInput" part="payload"
            query="/tns:EligibilityProcessRequest/tns:Account">
      </from>
      <to  part="parameters"
            query="/nsxml0:assessEligibility/nsxml0:Account"
            variable="webservice_account"/>
  </copy>
</assign>

<invoke name="CallEligibilityWebservice" partnerLink="EligibilityWebservice"
        portType="nsxml0:EligibilityService" operation=" assessEligibility "
        inputVariable="webservice_account"
        outputVariable="webservice_eligibilityResults"/>
```

Maintenance Phase

As for the maintenance phase—the longest phase of any project—moving business rules out of Java code and into the rules engine makes maintenance much more manageable. As I explained previously, business managers can modify rules at run time using a graphical interface, and business rules and BPEL processes can change independently of each other.

Executing JRules with Oracle BPEL Process Manager

Clearly, the design and development of rules, web services, and BPEL processes involve multiple different technologies. In this section, I will discuss how these technologies work together at run time to execute the Eligibility Process. Although this example is based on Oracle BPEL Process Manager and ILOG JRules specifically, it is applicable to many other environments.

The rules engine invocation occurs across three tiers (see figure opposite): BPEL invoking the rules web service, the rules web service invoking the rules engine, rules engine application code receiving input and returning results.

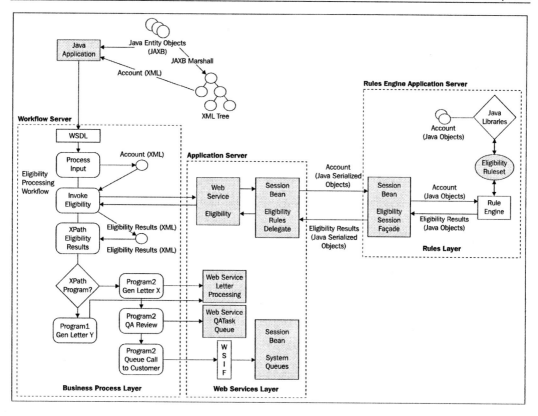

In the context of our example business process, the application invokes the Eligibility Process with an XML payload. This payload contains information about the account, such as family attributes. The Eligibility Process in turn invokes the Eligibility web service. The Eligibility web service provides the translation from XML to JAXB and then invokes the Eligibility Rules Delegate session bean. The latter interacts with the session façade using RMI. The session façade activates the rules engine, which then calculates and returns eligibility results to the process. The Eligibility Process will assess the return and assign either Program 1 or Program 2 to the account. In our example, we provide a remote server to run eligibility rules, but this could just as well be hosted locally. (Note that it is best practice not to co-locate non-process services with the BPEL Process Manager to allow for better scalability.)

This example effectively illustrates the separation of business logic into rules, BPEL, and web services:

- The Eligibility BPEL Process explicitly defines the steps that must be executed based on the received Eligibility Results data. Based on the Eligibility Results, the Eligibility BPEL Process will invoke different branches. Program 1 and 2 each executes different steps, and these steps can be easily modified using a BPEL designer.

- Eligibility Web services execute medium-grained tasks for the BPEL Process Manager, which encapsulates the mechanics of how to send correspondence and queue tasks. Web services operate on summary data from the common data model such as database keys (such as an Account OID) that can be used to extract detailed data to perform the required task.

- Eligibility rules do not modify the original data, nor do they access external data sources. The rules-engine auditing trail is trivial because you have the exact record of the data in/out of the rules.

The specifics of integrating rules into a J2EE platform via web services are illustrated in the figure below. Rules are deployed in a standalone EAR (EligiblityRules.ear) and registered with the rules engine admin console. The rest of the supporting logic is deployed in another EAR (EligibilityRuleService.ear), which includes the classes for the Account JAXB objects that EligibilityRules will require and the session façade to invoke the rules. The session façade hides the details of invoking the JRules custom libraries and also allows the system to be ported to a new rules engine provider.

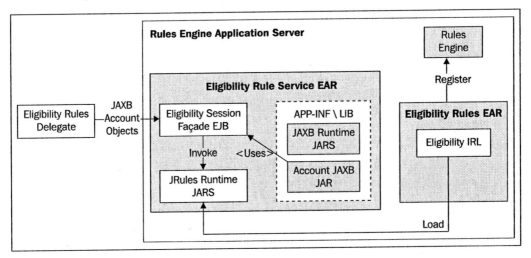

Conclusion

In this BPEL "recipe", I've presented a strategy for spreading business logic across three different layers: business process layer, web services layer, and rules layer. You can utilize these complementary technologies to minimize interdependencies between data and logic. However, to derive full benefits, the architect must perform a rigorous analysis to decompose the system components and design them using the appropriate technology. The development process involves multiple technologies and various roles. It is necessary to identify appropriate resources up front to participate in the development process. The resulting architecture is an agile platform on which business users handle most business changes without IT intervention.

5

Building Rich Internet Applications for Workflow and Process Monitoring

by Doug Todd

Create a real-time workflow and advanced process activity monitoring dashboard by extending Oracle BPEL Process Manager APIs.

More and more organizations are automating their key business processes to increase operational effectiveness. However, even automated processes require manual interaction for two important reasons: to advance a process to the next step (workflow), and to provide real-time process visibility for end users (process monitoring).

Consider a business process for opening a new bank account. First, the customer provides necessary details (name, address, SSN, initial deposit) to open the account. Once the process kicks-off, the customer will want to track the status of the request and respond to any additional queries from the bank. This process requires workflow to enable customer participation, and process monitoring so that the customer can track request status.

Oracle BPEL Process Manager facilitates basic workflow capabilities and process activity monitoring. But just as important, by extending its exhaustive API interfaces for interacting with processes, instances, and workflow, it is possible to build a single, **rich internet application (RIA)** that enables advanced workflow and process activity monitoring. This advanced workflow capability could enable zero-latency communications between user and process, whereas advanced process activity monitoring could transmit real-time process status information to the workflow so that appropriate actions could be taken.

In this chapter of *The BPEL Cookbook*, I will present a sample business scenario that requires real-time workflow and advanced process activity monitoring capability. We will then explore the architecture of a Macromedia Flex-based RIA that leverages the BPEL Process Manager API to meet those goals, and then learn how the RIA initiates processes and integrates workflow. You will also learn how to visually depict the process paths available as well as those actually taken by the current instance. (This functionality is very valuable when examining processes in retrospect.) Finally, you will get an introduction to audit trail tracking using the API interfaces.

RIA Background

An RIA is a hybrid of web application and traditional desktop application, typically built using "interactive" technologies including JavaScript, Flash, Java Applets, XML User Interface Markup Language (XUL), Extensible Application Markup Language (XAML), JavaServer Faces, and Swinglets, often using an Asynchronous XML and JavaScript (AJAX) approach. RIAs can potentially improve the usability and effectiveness of online applications as well as increase developer productivity. According to Gartner Research, by 2010, at least 60% of new application development projects will include RIA technology of some kind.

Our example here comprises a BPEL workflow interface and process monitoring console that offers end users a unified, feature-rich dashboard. Note that it is important to differentiate this application from the Oracle BPEL Console or true Business Activity Monitoring (BAM); although a certain level of functionality overlap exists, the RIA target user community is vastly different than that for the latter two applications. The BPEL Console is more suited for administrators and developers who debug, deploy, and maintain process instances, and BAM appeals to process owners (executives, LOB managers, and so on) and IT managers who want to measure key performance indicators (KPIs) and then take action to refine the process. In contrast, the example RIA application described here is designed with end users in mind: customers, partners, or suppliers who want to track the status of a specific business interaction and don't care about KPIs or process improvement.

Sample Process

The sample business process, "New Account Request", is a multi-organization process that creates accounts for a financial service intermediary, its financial partners (insurance companies and their financial advisors), mutual fund companies, and clearinghouses. Here we will focus on the first two steps of this process.

1. The process accepts the customer's SSN and then extracts and displays customer information (name, address) from the database.
2. The customer verifies this data, adds the deposit amount, and clicks on Submit.

Clearly customers will need a workflow interface to enter the SSN, verify name and address, and input the deposit amount. In addition, they will need the ability to visually monitor the progress of the request.

In the next section, I will offer an overview of the development aspects of building such an application. Later, you will see how the New Account business process executes using this application.

Building the Application

As explained previously, you will design this application with two primary goals:

*   Provide a rich unified user interface for users to track the process status and provide input as and when required (RIA front end)
*   Offer advanced process monitoring (BPEL Process Manager API back end)

RIA Front End

The RIA user interface is the "face" of the application; it runs and manages the New Account business process. This presentation layer is built using Macromedia Flex technology and the ActionScript scripting language. It accepts the user input and passes it to the BPEL process. It also displays the current status of the process.

The following figure shows the RIA front end for the New Account business process:

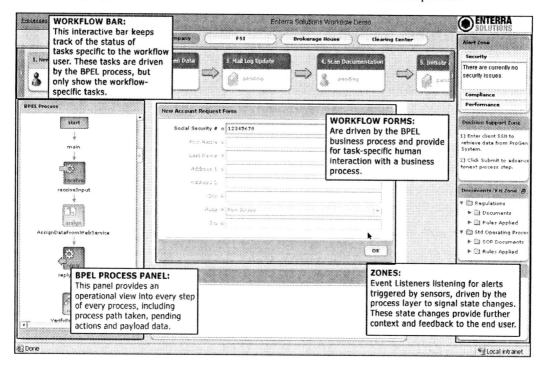

Let's review its four main components and their key capabilities:

- **Workflow Bar:** The Workflow Bar allows the user to view the workflow steps in the New Account process at the business level. Every step in the Workflow Bar is exploded in the BPEL Panel.

- **BPEL Panel:** The BPEL Process Panel offers an exploded view of every step of the New Account process. The panel dynamically reads the process model and the instance audit trail of a given process instance to combine the process paths available with the paths actually taken by the current instance. The panel also polls the audit trail to determine what action is pending, visually delineating where the current process is at that time. Any nodes of the process previously executed can be clicked on to view their respective payload. This functionality gives operations and compliance managers real-time visibility into the past, current, and potential future state of the current process.

- **Workflow Forms:** Workflow Forms correspond to the workflow steps within the New Account BPEL process. This Flex "view stack" communicates with the audit trail of the business process, changing the view stack form to match the context of the BPEL process.

- **Zones:** Zones provides alerts and feedback to assist the workflow and process activity users perform their respective jobs (not discussed here).

These panels offer superior usability experience and interact with the BPEL API. Now let's see which back end API functions are leveraged to execute the RIA front end.

BPEL Process Manager API Back End

The BPELService class facilitates interaction between the RIA front end and the process activity monitoring capabilities in the BPEL Process Manager API. As shown in the figure that follows and described in the subsequent table, BPELservice uses five interfaces within the BPEL Process Manager API for process, process instances, and tasks to deliver on the promise of workflow-enabled process activity management and monitoring.

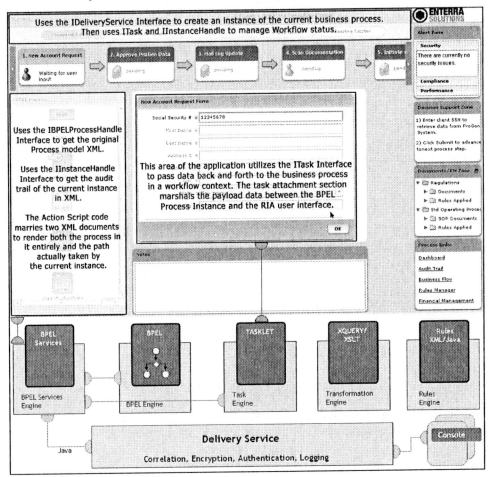

Interface	Allows the user to...
IDeliveryService	Invoke instances from processes deployed on a BPEL process domain
IBPELProcessHandle	Explore a BPEL process deployed on a BPEL process domain
IInstanceHandle	Perform operations on an active instance
ITask	Interact with a task that has been instantiated in a process domain
IWorklistService	Search for and complete tasks that have been instantiated from the process domain

Now that you understand the basic components of RIA and BPELService, let's see how they work together to offer a rich end-user experience.

Running the New Account Process

As explained previously, the customer is first presented with an input screen in the workflow panel to enter the SSN. As soon as the user clicks on Submit, a "New Account Application" XML document is created using ActionScript and passed to the BPELService server-side Java class via Flex's Remote Object Architecture. (This enables Flex to speak directly to Java objects such as BPELService.) The Java component uses an instance of the IDeliveryService interface to initiate the BPEL process. The initiateProcess Java method, shown below, then returns the instance reference ID of the newly created business process instance to the Flex client. This reference ID is used in subsequent operations for targeting the correct business process instance.

```
/**
 * This function initiates an instance of a BPEL PM process based on the
 * process name. The function sets the function id and the reference id for
 * future use.
 *
 * @param xmlRequest
 *              is the initiating request message for the process
 * @param strBusinessProcess
 *              the business process name
 * @return the initiating response message for the process
 */
public String initiateProcess(Document xmlRequest, String strBusinessProcess)
{
    System.out.println("Initiate" + strBusinessProcess);
    /*
     * This interface allows users to invoke instances from processes
     * deployed on a BPEL process domain.
     */
    IDeliveryService deliveryService = getDeliveryService();
    /*
     * Construct the normalized message and send to Oracle BPEL process
     * manager
     */
    NormalizedMessage nm = new NormalizedMessage();
    nm.addPart(PAYLOAD, xmlRequest.getDocumentElement());

    NormalizedMessage responseNm = null;
    try {
        responseNm = deliveryService.request(strBusinessProcess, PROCESS,
        nm);
```

```
        } catch (Exception e) {
                e.printStackTrace();
                throw new RuntimeException("Could not initialize process.");
        }
        Map payload = responseNm.getPayload();
        Document xmlResponse = getXMLDoc(
                XMLHelper.elementToString((Element) payload.get(PAYLOAD)));
        /*
         * Sets the Instance reference ID for integrating active BPEL
         * instances.
         */
        setInstanceReferenceId(strBusinessProcess, xmlResponse);

        return XMLHelper.elementToString(xmlResponse.getDocumentElement());
}
```

Enabling Workflow

As shown in the following figure, customer data is retrieved from an external system via the BPEL process and presented in the workflow panel. The user then verifies the data, enters the deposit amount, and clicks on OK.

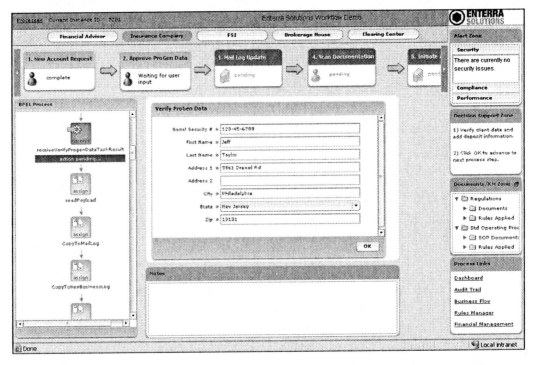

The workflow capabilities are based on the ITask and IWorklistService interfaces provided by BPEL Process Manager. The RIA correlates the tasks in the IWorklistService with the workflow screen needed to complete the given task. When proper form validation has occurred, the user interface makes a remote object call to the completeTask method, shown next, to send the data captured in the UI to the BPEL process for further processing.

```
/**
* This function gets the user input from workflow zone, relates it to a task
* and completes the task. The function uses instance reference id for
* identifying process instance.
*/

public String completeTask(String strInstanceReferenceID,
    String strActivityLabel, Document payload) {
    System.out.println("completeTask-" + strInstanceReferenceID + "-"
    + strActivityLabel);
    String strStatus = "OK";
    try {
        IWorklistService worklist = getWorklist();
        // get task reference
        ITask task = getTask(strInstanceReferenceID, strActivityLabel);

        // set task payload
        task.setAttachment(payload.getDocumentElement());

        worklist.completeTask(task);

    } catch (Exception e) {
            e.printStackTrace();
            strStatus = ERROR_STRING;
    }
    return strStatus;
}
```

The code places the task-specific data into the task attachment provided by the ITask interface. This interface not only sends the pertinent data back to the BPEL process, but also places that data into the BPEL process audit trail.

Next, I'll introduce the other important aspect of your RIA application: process monitoring.

Monitoring Process Activity

During the first two steps discussed earlier—initiating the process and enabling the workflow—process states are visually updated via IProcessHandle and IInstanceHandle API interfaces.

Oracle BPEL Console provides a web-based interface for deploying, managing, administering, and debugging BPEL processes. It's an administrative tool designed using JSP pages and servlets that call the BPEL Process Manager API. Consequently, you can easily develop your own RIA console using the API to provide a business-level, process-monitoring interface.

This console provides visual feedback for a specific instance of a process and even provides a link into the audit trail data associated with a given step in a process. However, the primary advantage of the RIA console lies in its ability to perform actual versus planned analysis. The console displays all the possible steps a process could take during its execution; it also renders the path that was in fact taken during execution. Users can click on any process node to retrieve the BPEL payload and render the payload information in a dialog box.

Thanks to visually demarcated ideal-versus-actual process paths and the ability to drill down at the payload level, end users can analyze the process and identify the trouble spots on their own, without IT intervention. The following figure depicts an example of actual-versus-ideal process path analysis; the "actual" path is haloed in green (since the figure is in grayscale, the path has been highlighted using a box).

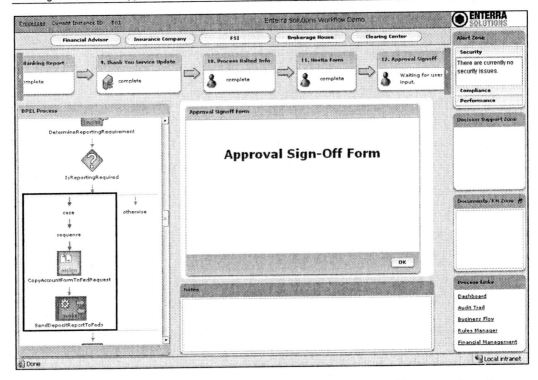

Next we'll examine how processes are rendered to enable this analysis and how to retrieve the audit trail data and depict it visually within an RIA application.

Rendering the Process

The Flex BPEL Panel component makes calls to the IProcessHandle interface to retrieve the XML representation of the business model in its entirety. The BPEL Panel uses the IInstanceHandle interface to gather the XML representation of the current instance's audit trail. The BPEL Panel then compares and merges the two XML representations to create a user interface that can portray the entire model and the path taken.

Flex is particularly adept at such operations by virtue of its native XML capabilities. Flex can easily merge two XML representations by using a combination of Flex repeater controls and ActionScripts. Together, they have the ability to convert XML into an array and then utilize the inherent array-handling capabilities to facilitate the merging of the XML.

The Process Model XML actually serves as the basis for the BPEL Panel as it contains all possible nodes. With each step of the Process Model, the Process model ID is compared to the audit trail model ID. When the IDs of the process and audit match, the results of that node are copied from the audit model into the process model. Determining what path was taken is as simple as interrogating which nodes in the model have actual instance data associated with them.

The following code snippets show the `getProcessModel` and `getInstanceAuditTrail` methods.

`getProcessModel` method:

```
/**
* This function gets the debugger XML model of a given BPEL process.
*
* The function returns the xml model.
*
*
* @param strProcessID
*              the business process name.
* @return the xml process model.
*/
public String getProcessModel(String strProcessID) {
    System.out.println("getProcessModel - " + strProcessID);
    String strProcessModel = "";
    try {
        IBPELProcessHandle process = getLocator().lookupProcess(
                strProcessID);
        // Returns the debugger XML model of this BPEL process.
        strProcessModel = process.getProcessModel();
    } catch (Exception e) {
            e.printStackTrace();
            strProcessModel = ERROR_STRING;
    }
    return strProcessModel;
}
```

`getInstanceAuditTrail` method:

```
/**
* This function gets the XML audit trail of a given BPEL process.
*
* The function returns the xml model.
*
*
* @param strProcessID
*              the business process name.
* @return the xml process model.
*/
public String getInstanceAuditTrail(String strInstanceReferenceID) {
    System.out.println("getInstanceAuditTrail - " + strInstanceReferenceID);
    String strResponse = "";
    try {
        IInstanceHandle instance = getInstance(strInstanceReferenceID);
        // Returns the XML representation of the audit trail of this
        // instance.
        strResponse = instance.getAuditTrail();
    } catch (Exception e) {
            e.printStackTrace();
            strResponse = ERROR_STRING;
    }
    return strResponse;
}
```

Viewing Audit Trail Data

Audit trail data is available to each node of a process that has already executed. This functionality is similar to that in the BPEL Console. The Flex user interface accesses the *details data* for the node of the process chosen in the user interface (see the following figure):

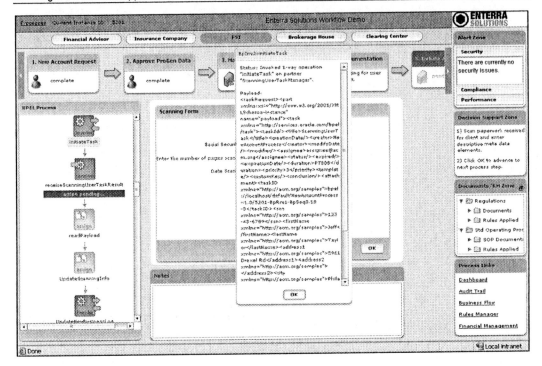

Audit trail data can be extracted using the following ActionScript 2.0 code:

```
bpelObject.bpelDetails = eventData.event.details.data;
```

The Flex interface polls for changes in the status of the current business process by tracking activity in the audit trail to visually delineate what step is pending in the business process. When a change is detected, the Flex application requests a new current instance trace using a remoting call to retrieve the audit trail. The instance trace is then used to display data on the input screens associated with each BPEL process user task. Flex client input screens are associated with corresponding BPEL process steps using activity Correlation IDs.

Conclusion

The value of a business process lies in its ability to offer superior visual depiction of process performance and enable task integration. The application described here offers tremendous aesthetic appeal to end users.

As I've demonstrated, RIAs can offer a loosely-coupled presentation-tier approach for delivering new SOA applications. By combining an RIA front end with an SOA back end, enterprises can lower the management and deployment costs of internet applications.

6

Building BPEL Processes on the Fly

by Jerry Thomas

Generate BPEL processes on the fly by transforming parameters stored in the database into a BPEL XML definition file via XQuery.

In Chapter 7 of this cookbook, you will learn how to make BPEL processes dynamic by manipulating partner links using end-point references. This approach is certainly useful for building processes that are shielded from partner relationship changes. However, in many processes, various other variables in addition to the partner links may need to change dynamically.

Consider a company that has designed a workplace-management solution for managing corporate real estate and facilities that help clients answer the following types of questions.

- How much space are different business units using? How can business units share space most efficiently?

- When will property leases expire? By looking at the company's growth trajectory, how should leases be renegotiated?

- How can we best plan and approve a move of a business unit to a different floor, or expand into a building across the street?

The workplace-management solution automates business processes such as tracking the occupancy of an office cubicle and disassociating that space from the business unit if it has been unoccupied for three months. As the company deploys this process for different clients, it becomes imperative to tailor the process to their business needs—one company might prefer to send an email to the property manager before the cube is taken away from the business unit, whereas another might prefer to wait a longer period before taking any action.

In this situation, creating a business process from scratch for every client would represent a major investment in time, money, and resources. And creating a reusable business process would require a deep understanding of BPEL constructs.

In contrast, adaptive business processes could be quickly customized per the varying requirements of specific organizations, enabling faster automation, reducing development costs, and accelerating time to market. In this approach, you would hide the complexities of BPEL and enable analysts to model business processes that are as similar to "real life" as possible.

This process requires a custom business-process designer, however, that allows analysts to represent business flow without worrying about the complexities of BPEL. This custom designer stores the definition of the process within the database. Every time the process needs to be updated, a business analyst uses the custom designer to update the process accordingly.

In essence, once the process definition is loaded into the database, BPEL processes can be constructed "on the fly" from there. This newly constructed business process can in turn be deployed dynamically.

Oracle BPEL Process Manager is an ideal tool for this approach; it works seamlessly with third-party designers and provides the ability to deploy BPEL processes dynamically. For example, my company, CenterStone Software, leverages this approach to provide a solution to rapidly automate workplace business processes and manage corporate real estate and facilities. Our eCenterOne application uses Oracle BPEL to quickly let property managers develop and deploy custom business processes.

In this chapter, I'll explain how a custom BPEL designer stores process definitions in the database. After reviewing the database schema to store the definition, you will create a BPEL file on the fly from a sample business process using XQuery and the Saxon XQuery parser (http://saxon.sourceforge.net/). Finally, you will learn how to deploy this process dynamically using an Ant script.

The Approach

As I explained previously, the ability to build processes on the fly offers significant benefits. The following figure shows the entire lifecycle of the business process created on the fly:

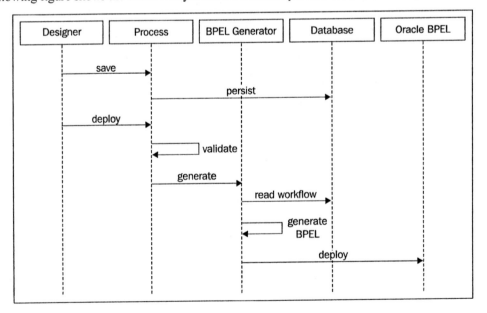

Building on-the-fly processes comprises several steps:

1. An analyst uses a custom designer to graphically model the business process.

2. The process definition is stored in the database by the custom designer.

3. The BPEL Generator reads and validates the process definition. It then generates the BPEL XML file from the database representation as well as associated files used for deployment.

4. The BPEL process is dynamically deployed on the Oracle BPEL Process Manager Server.

Let's use the following sample business scenario to walk through each step.

Sample Business Scenario

Consider the sample real-estate management business process described previously. This "Cube Management" business process involves the following activities:

1. Initiate a business process when an office cube is emptied (the EmployeeCount field for a space is set to 0 (zero)).

2. Wait for three months (if the space's EmployeeCount is set higher than 0, exit the flow).

3. Send email to the property manager that the space is no longer being charged to its original business unit.

4. Update the space so that it no longer belongs to its original business unit.

Process Creation

Process creation is the first step for building processes on the fly. Generally, processes are modeled using Oracle Designer or Eclipse Designer and BPEL files are generated automatically.

In our approach, you will replace a conventional IDE with a custom designer. Also, instead of creating a BPEL file directly, you will store the definition inside a database.

The following figure shows how the sample business process is modeled in the designer:

As I described previously, the Oracle BPEL Process Manager engine has the unique capability to integrate with any designer/tool, provided the latter can generate valid BPEL files.

Storing the Definition in the Database

Once the business process has been created, the next step is to store the definition inside the database. Your database schema must be sufficiently flexible to store complex processes and allow for re-creation of BPEL processes with multiple BPEL constructs such as flow, pick, invoke, and scope.

Assume that you have designed a data model containing business process design information that corresponds to the real-life view provided by the custom designer. When a business analyst creates a business process using the designer, information defining the structure of the business process is saved to the database. Note that Oracle BPEL Process Manager does not come into play until deployment (more on that later).

The following figure contains a high-level UML view of the data model used to persist process designs in our database:

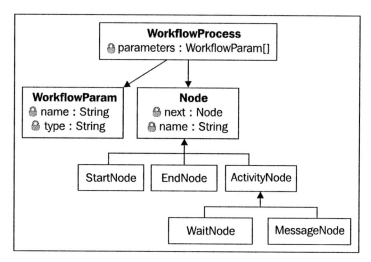

The workflowProcess object stores the process design; it contains parameters and nodes, which define the sequence and type of activities in the process. The various workflowNode objects are design-time artifacts for the different types of process activities supported by your designer. Note that these are not BPEL constructs; rather, they are custom constructs that are then mapped to typically more than one BPEL activity. Once deployed using custom designer, the CubeManagement process details will be stored as follows in the database.

WorkflowProcess Table:

Name	ID
CubeManagement	1

WorkflowParameter Table:

WorkflowProcess_ID	Name	Type
1	CubeParam	Space

WorkflowNode Table:

Workflow Process _ID	Node Id	Next Node	Type	E-mail	Parame ter_ID	Update Field	Updat eValue	Wait Time
1	1	2	Start					
1	2	3	Wait					3 months
1	3	4	Message	max@big.com				

Workflow Process _ID	Node Id	Next Node	Type	E-mail	Parame ter_ID	Update Field	Updat eValue	Wait Time
1	4	5	Update		1	businessUnit	null	
1	5	null	End					

These tables are read by the BPEL Generator to dynamically generate a BPEL file. The next section describes that process.

Dynamically Deploying BPEL

The most complex task in BPEL generation involves reading the process design from the database and generating a BPEL "suitcase" for the process. In this example, you will leverage XQuery to generate BPEL.

XQuery is a powerful and convenient language for processing XML data. It can handle not only files in XML format, but also database data whose structure—nested, with named trees and attributes—is similar to XML.

The following files, which make up a BPEL process suitcase for Oracle BPEL Process Manager, are generated dynamically:

BPEL file	This XML file is the actual business process; it follows the BPEL specification.
WSDL files	Web Service WSDL files describe two interfaces:
	• The interface exposed by your BPEL process hosted in Oracle BPEL Process Manager. This interface is fairly simple, involving a call to start a process instance along with a callback interface.
	• The interface exposed by eCenterOne. For simplicity, this too involves a single interface that can be used to handle any call from the process running in Oracle BPEL Process Manager to our server as well as an associated callback.
`bpel.xml`	A deployment descriptor XML file that describes the BPEL process to Oracle BPEL Process Manager.
	It holds process settings with information specific to Oracle BPEL Process Manager and the following information:
	• Location information specifying the location of the eCenterOne web service
	• Information specifying how retries should be performed should calls to eCenterOne fail (retries)
`Ant build.xml`	Uses Oracle BPEL Process Manager's `bpelc` Ant task to deploy the BPEL process (more on that later).

Here we will focus only on how the BPEL file is generated dynamically. This process involves iterating across the nodes stored in the database and generating corresponding BPEL activities for each node:

1. **Iterate across the database**. BPEL generation is implemented in Java code that reads each workflow node for a workflow process and creates a list of all the nodes to be processed.

2. **Create BPEL Activity for each node**. Each workflow node in the list is generated into a number of BPEL activities that are enclosed in a `<scope/>` activity. Consequently, if the processing for a BPEL activity requires use of a BPEL parameter, that parameter is only visible within that scope (no variable name collisions, and so on). For each node, you must create an XQuery template to generate a corresponding BPEL XML tag. The XQuery processor will process the XQuery template to construct the BPEL with node and instance information and pass back the result.

3. **Create BPEL file**. The calling process combines BPEL activities for each node and creates a master BPEL file, which represents the entire process. The `<scope/>` blocks generated for each workflow node can simply be appended to each other in the following manner:

```
<process>
  <scope>
    <!- start workflow node related activities -!>
  </scope>
  <scope>
    <!- wait workflow node related activities -!>
  </scope>
  <scope>
    <!- mail workflow node related activities -!>
  </scope>
  <scope>
    <!- update workflow node related activities -!>
  </scope>
</process>
```

Let's analyze Step 2 in greater detail. Every node equates to a series of BPEL activities. All this information is stored in the XQuery template file. There is an XQuery template for each node, which embodies all the BPEL constructs for that specific node. You have created `start.xq`, `wait.xq`, `message.xq`, `update.xq`, and `stop.xq`, corresponding to five nodes in the Cube Management process.

The following table describes the BPEL activities generated for `start`, `wait`, `message`, `update`, and end nodes in the example process:

Nodes in Cube Management Process	Equivalent BPEL Constructs
start	`<sequence>`
	`<receive>`
	`<assign>`
	`<scope>`

Nodes in Cube Management Process	Equivalent BPEL Constructs			
			`<variables>`	
			`<sequence>`	
				`<assign>`
				`<invoke>`
wait	`<scope>`			
		`<variables>`		
		`<sequence>`		
			`<assign>`	
			`<invoke>`	
			`<pick>`	
message	`<scope>`			
		`<variables>`		
		`<sequence>`		
			`<assign>`	
			`<invoke>`	
update	`<scope>`			
		`<variables>`		
		`<sequence>`		
			`<assign>`	
			`<invoke>`	
end	`<scope>`			
		`<variables>`		
		`<sequence>`		
			`<assign>`	
			`<invoke>`	
			`<terminate>`	

Note how each process node is generated into a hierarchy of BPEL activities. For example, the BPEL used to generate the message activity looks like this (it is stored in an XQuery file `message.xq`):

```
declare namespace ent = "http://www.centerstonesoft.com/schema/entity";
declare variable $nodeKey as xs:string external;
<scope>
  <!-- generation for Message activity -->
  <variables>

  <!-- Define variables input, output and error variables-->
    <variable name="emailRequest"
          messageType="services:EntityAsyncMsgWSRequestMessage"/>
      <variable name="emailResponse"
          messageType="services:EntityAsyncMsgWSResultMessage"/>
```

```
      <variable name="fault" messageType="services:EntityFaultMessage" />
</variables>

<!--Begin the BPEL activities -->
<sequence>

<!--This is the first assign activity. It configures the input variable with
<!-- identification of node ($nodekey) and function to be called -->
<!-- by the external webService (bpelSendEmail). -->

  <assign>
    <copy>
      <from>
        <ent:EntityCollectionElem
            xmlns:ent="http://www.centerstonesoft.com/schema/entity" >
          <ent:Header/>
          <ent:entityName/>
          <ent:EntityElem>
            <ent:entityKey>{ $nodeKey }</ent:entityKey>
            <ent:method >
              <ent:methodName>bpelSendEmail</ent:methodName>
              <ent:parameter>
                <ent:PropName>thread</ent:PropName>
                <ent:Type>string</ent:Type>
                <ent:Value/>
              </ent:parameter>
            </ent:method>
          </ent:EntityElem>
        </ent:EntityCollectionElem>
      </from>
      <to variable="emailRequest" part="payload"/>
    </copy>
  </assign>

<!--Second and third assign activity configure the input variable -->
<!--with identification of actual process instance -->

  <assign>
    <copy>
      <from variable="input" part="parameters" query="//ent:Header"/>
      <to variable="emailRequest" part="payload" query="//ent:Header"/>
    </copy>
  </assign>
  <assign>
    <copy>
      <from variable="threadKey" part="value"/>
      <to variable="emailRequest" part="payload"
          query="//ent:parameter[ent:PropName = 'thread']/ent:Value"/>
    </copy>
  </assign>

<!--After configuring input variable with node, instance and function to
    be called, invoke the external service -->
<invoke name="invoke" partnerLink="EntityAsyncMsgWSLink"
        portType="services:EntityAsyncMsgWS" operation="invoke"
        inputVariable="emailRequest"/>

<!--Check response from external service. If response indicates fault,
    throw exception. -->
<!--If no response is received for 10 days, throw exception -->
<pick name="deadlined_receive" >

<!--Set output variable if return result from external webservice is OK-->
```

```
            <onMessage partnerLink="EntityAsyncMsgWSLink"
                    portType="services:EntityAsyncMsgWSCallback"
                    operation="onResult" variable="emailResponse">
                <empty/>
            </onMessage>

        <!--On fault, check the fault code and throw  appropriate exception-->

            <onMessage operation="onFault" partnerLink="EntityAsyncMsgWSLink"
                    portType="services:EntityAsyncMsgWSCallback"
                    variable="fault">
                <switch>
                    <case condition="bpws:getVariableData('fault', 'value',
                        '/EntityFault/faultcode') = 'MailException' ">
                        <throw faultName="ent:MailException" faultVariable="fault" />
                    </case>
                    <otherwise>
                        <throw faultName="ent:SystemException" faultVariable="fault" />
                    </otherwise>
                </switch>
            </onMessage>

            <!--If no response for 10 days, throw  exception-->
            <onAlarm  for="'P10D'">
                <throw faultName="ent:SystemException"/>
            </onAlarm>
        </pick>
    </sequence>
</scope>
```

After reviewing this XQuery template, you'll see how the document generates a single <scope> activity that contains the implementation of the message process node. The <scope> activity begins with a <variables> section where variables are defined for the request as well a normal response or fault response. The variables section is followed by a <sequence> where the request is generated using a sequence of <assign> statements. The first <assign> writes the boilerplate for the request; within this <assign>, the XQuery parameter nodeKey is used to pass node identification to the external web service.

Note that nodeKey is generation-time information. After the first <assign> activity, the following two <assign> activities deal with run-time information. The second <assign> copies header information from the initial request used to start the process. This header information identifies the eCenterOne and Oracle BPEL Process Manager process-instance IDs as well as the customer that the process is for. The third <assign> activity copies the process thread ID. (As mentioned earlier, similar XQuery templates exist for other nodes in the process.)

XQuery Processing

Let's quickly look at how all these templates are processed by the XQuery processor and combined to form a BPEL file.

The generateActivity() method that follows accepts the list of nodes for which the BPEL activities need to be generated. For each node, it will locate the right XQuery template using the xQuery.newXQueryFromResource function. The Saxon processor will then process this XQuery template and produce an XML string. If a node has a child, it will be processed in a recursive manner in the while loop.

```
/**
 * Recursively generates an activity including any child activities.
 * @param activity the node that is being generated, the value is null for the
 * top-level process node
 * @return typically the root element of the generated XML document
 * @throws EntityException
 */
    protected String generateActivity(WorkflowNode activity) throws
EntityException
        {
    //Find the next node in the list to be processed
        BpelActivityType activityType = getBpeBpelActivityType(activity);
    //Get the parameters to be passed to node
        HashMap params = calculateParameters(activity, activityType);
        try {
            //Get corresponding XQuery file for the node
            XQuery q = XQuery.newXQueryFromResource("bpelgen/" +
                        activityType.getQuery());
            //Call the Saxon XQuery Processor to run the query.
            XQueryResult result = q.run(null, params, null);
            //Convert the result into a string
            String parentXml = result.serializeString();
            if (logger.isDebugEnabled()) {
                logger.debug("Generated for parent '" + activityType.getName()
                            + "' is \n" + parentXml);
            }
            //If there are child nodes, recursively invoke generate activity
            if (_process.hasChildren(activity)) {
                //Call java relational class
                Iterator it = _process.getChildrenIterator(activity);
                //Recursively call generateActivity for child nodes.
                //For 'Cube Management Process', these will be
                //start, wait, message, update & end
                while (it.hasNext()) {
                    WorkflowNode childActivity = (WorkflowNode) it.next();
                    String childXml = generateActivity(childActivity);
                    // now use Saxon XSLT to add the document generated for
                    // the children to the result document
                    // Get the Transformer used for this transformation
                    Transformer transformer = getPrependTransformer();
                    transformer.setParameter("inserted", DomUtils.getDocument(
                            new ByteArrayInputStream(childXml.getBytes())));
                    StreamResult saveResult = new StreamResult(
                                            new ByteArrayOutputStream());
                    try {
                        StreamSource src = new StreamSource(
                            new ByteArrayInputStream(parentXml.getBytes()));
                        // Transform the XML Source
                        transformer.transform(src, saveResult);
                    }
                    finally {
                        transformer.clearParameters();
                    }
                    parentXml =
            ((ByteArrayOutputStream)saveResult.getOutputStream()).toString();
                    if (logger.isDebugEnabled()) {
                        BpelActivityType childType =
                                    getBpeBpelActivityType(childActivity);
                        logger.debug("Preprocessed for parent '" +
                                activityType.getName() + "' and child '" +
                                childType.getName() + "' is \n" +
                                parentXml);
                    }
                }
            }
        }
```

```
                    // remove the <insert-here> node
                    Transformer transformer = getRemovePrependTransformer();
                    StreamResult saveResult = new StreamResult(
                                                new ByteArrayOutputStream());
                    StreamSource src = new StreamSource(
                                    new ByteArrayInputStream(parentXml.getBytes()));
                    transformer.transform(src, saveResult);
                    parentXml =
                      ((ByteArrayOutputStream)saveResult.getOutputStream()).toString();
                    if (logger.isDebugEnabled()) {
                        logger.debug("Generated for '"+activityType.getName()+
                                        "' is \n" + parentXml);
                    }
                    return parentXml;
                }
                catch (SAXException ex) {
                    throw new EntityException("Failed to run transform "+
                                            activityType.getQuery(), ex);
                }
                catch (TransformerException ex) {
                    throw new EntityException("Failed to run transform "+
                                            activityType.getQuery(), ex);
                }
                catch (IOException ex) {
                    throw new EntityException("Failed to load query "+
                                            activityType.getQuery(), ex);
                }
        }
```

The generateActivity() method generates the final BPEL file in a string format. It is then written into a file by another Java program. All XQuery templates as well as the BPEL file for the Cube Management process are available for download as the sample code.

Dynamic Deployment with Ant

The final step is to use Oracle BPEL Process Manager deployment tools to compile and deploy the BPEL process. For deployment, you need to generate the following simple Ant build.xml file and then execute it (again using XQuery for its support of parameterized XML files).

```
<?xml version="1.0" encoding="UTF-8"?>
<project default="main"
 basedir="C:/DOCUME~1/jerry/LOCALS~1/Temp/cs_bpelgen_simple24369"
 name="BpelDeploy">
    <target name="main">
        <bpelc keepGenerated="true" deploy="jt_dev" rev="1.0"
         home="c:\orabpel"/>
    </target>
</project>
```

The final step is to execute Ant programmatically from your application server. To do this, you can use code from the Ant task Execute (found in org.apache.tools.ant.taskdefs). This class provides industrial-strength support for programmatically executing command-line processes and handling good and error returns.

The following code fragment describes how to use code in the Ant Execute task to implement BPEL process deployment:

```
String args[] = new String[1];
args[0] = "c:/orabpelpm/integration/orabpel/bin/obant.bat";
```

```
Execute exe = new Execute();
exe.setCommandline(args);
exe.setWorkingDirectory(_deploydir);
int retval = exe.execute();
if ( retval != 0 ) {
    throw new ExecuteException("process failed to deploy"); ...
```

In this fragment, the Execute class is used to execute the Oracle BPEL Process Manager command-line file, obant, directly. The batch file sets up the Windows environment appropriately and then invokes Ant on the build.xml file shown earlier.

A non-zero return code from this file is usually due to errors returned by the BPEL compiler. These errors are uncommon, however, and nearly always due to some internal error in the process implementation.

Conclusion

CenterStone Software lets property managers rapidly customize business processes using a custom designer. These processes are then dynamically converted into BPEL and deployed on Oracle BPEL Server. This approach should be seriously considered by any organization relying heavily on business users to design organizational processes. Not only does the custom designer approach shield users from the complexities of BPEL, but it also provides a unique platform to generate adaptive BPEL process on the fly. This enables organizations to enable and realize the benefits of SOA rapidly.

7

Making BPEL Processes Dynamic

by Sean Carey

Learn how to achieve dynamic binding by manipulating end-point references at run time.

Web services and service-oriented architecture (SOA) allow business processes to be easily extended through interaction with other business processes and applications. BPEL processes define this interaction through partner links, which define the interface (messages and operations), transport protocol, and most important, the location of each service to be used.

In most basic process designs, partner links are static; they refer to a single external process selected by the developer at design time. This approach is appropriate for highly targeted or constrained systems. However, in larger systems business processes are more complex. They interact with multiple external services and define multiple partner links, and some of these partner links might not be known at design time. As a result, all potential callouts and logic for deciding which partner links to use must be built inside the business process itself—unnecessarily complicating that process. Furthermore, as additional partner links are added, the resulting process grows more and more unwieldy, as any changes to the partner links require modification of the entire business process.

Fortunately, the BPEL language supports the concept of **dynamic binding** of partner links. Dynamic binding allows the developer to add new services through configuration or run-time inputs. This approach eliminates the need to anticipate and manage all parent-child relationships at design time.

In this chapter of *The BPEL Cookbook*, I will outline the effective strategy of shielding BPEL processes from partner relationship changes by letting the system manage partner links dynamically at run time. I will also explain how to invoke multiple BPEL processes dynamically, either sequentially or in parallel.

Dynamic Binding Overview

Similar to object-oriented analysis and design in the traditional programming world, dynamic binding of partner links allows for modularization of code and run-time binding between processes.

The benefits of this approach include:

- Support for team-oriented development by breaking down functional components into individual units of work

- Creation and deployment of additional sub-process components without the need to modify and redeploy parent processes

- Less need to use, maintain, and enhance individual overlapping processes

- Changes and enhancements to sub-processes are automatically accessible to parent processes

In essence, dynamic processes allow the system to adapt to conditions that would not otherwise be known at design time. For example, process flow can be determined by data content—if the data is insufficient, external data sources such as a relational database can be invoked at run time to determine process flow.

The use of dynamic processing can also have a significant advantage in organizations where there is a division of responsibility between development, and configuration and maintenance of high-level process flow. The development team can be responsible for understanding the details of the BPEL implementation and creation of the process components, and then domain experts such as business analysts or support teams can assemble these components into individual workflows without needing detailed knowledge of partner links, namespaces, WSDL, XPATH, and other technical details.

Building Dynamic BPEL Processes

As I explained previously, partner links describe interfaces to business processes or other services. BPEL processes call these external services using information stored in the partner links.

The partner link defines operations and message types that make up the interface to the service using port types in WSDL. As illustrated in the figure below, port types also indirectly define the transport used to communicate with the service (bindings) and the location of the service (services).

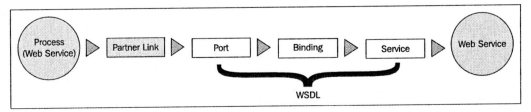

In a static BPEL process, the partner link information is defined at design time. However, there are scenarios where all the partner-link information is not known to the developer or needs to change at run time to adapt to data or other dynamic requirements.

Consider the example of a loan-processing scenario where you want to select the loan provider based on input data like geographic region, loan amount, or credit history. This data is not available until runtime, and if many possible loan providers are involved, it may be difficult to model the process to manage all the different services available to you statically.

Selecting the providers dynamically eliminates this problem. The WS-Addressing standard provides a mechanism called **endpoint references** that allows you to select one of the available services in the WSDL, or even define new services at run time. The business process is statically dependent on the interface information defined in the port type whereas an endpoint reference (which maps the binding to the service) allows you to redefine the service location dynamically. In essence, the endpoint reference is a dynamic alternative to the static service element defined in the WSDL. In many cases, the process designer can remain isolated from the decision about which services to call as long as those services all conform to a standard interface.

A good starting point for understanding these topics is the DynamicPartnerLink sample provided with Oracle BPEL Process Manager. Let's explore that sample step by step; then, you'll learn how to build a dynamic process from scratch. (I recommend that you become familiar with the standard LoanFlow tutorial before working with this sample.)

Understanding the DynamicPartnerLink Sample

The DynamicPartnerLink sample is a great resource for understanding the underlying concepts of partner links and endpoint references. It allows you to specify one of three loan service providers (United, Star, and American) and makes a dynamic call to the appropriate service based on the process input.

For this discussion you will be using the sample provided in the GA release of Oracle BPEL Process Manager 10.1.2; you will find it in directory `[BPEL_HOME]\samples\references\ DynamicPartnerLink`. I developed and tested the code discussed here under Patch 1 of version 10.1.2.

When you first load and deploy the DynamicPartnerLink sample, do not make any modifications to the code in the Oracle JDeveloper visual designer—just deploy it as-is. If you were to make and save such changes, JDeveloper would reformat the BPEL code based on its standard XML layout by introducing newline characters.

JDeveloper modifies the `<Address>` and `<ServiceName>` tags inside the `<EndpointReference>` data, adding a newline character before the `</Address>` and `</ServiceName>` closing tags. The newline appended to the data inside these elements breaks the binding. If necessary, you can correct the problem by removing the newline character before the closing tag on the service and address. Later I will present an alternative method for populating the endpoint reference that is not affected by the formatting applied by JDeveloper.

When you launch the sample from the console, you are asked for the standard loan application data for the loan flow demo (SSN, email, and so on) along with a provider field. Specify one of the following values for the provider string: united, american, or star. Run the sample with each of them to see how it works. The process will dynamically make calls to the appropriate loan provider. It is also interesting to try it with some other value in the provider string, as well as with no value at all.

To understand how this dynamic process works, it is first necessary to analyze the `DynamicPartnerLink.bpel` file. The first thing of interest in this file is the loan service partner link:

```
<partnerLink name="LoanService" partnerLinkType="services:LoanService"
    myRole="LoanServiceRequester" partnerRole="LoanServiceProvider"/>
```

Rather than defining a specific loan service (like `UnitedLoan`), a generic loan service name and type is specified (`services:LoanService`). The `LoanService` partner link is defined in the `LoanService.wsdl` file; this file is imported by adding it to the `bpel.xml` file in the `<partnerLinkBindings>` section as shown in the following snippet:

```
<partnerLinkBinding name="LoanService">
    <property name="wsdlLocation">LoanService.wsdl</property>
</partnerLinkBinding>
```

You'll observe in the `LoanService.wsdl` file that each of the available loan providers is defined as a `<service>` within this single WSDL file, as shown here:

```
<service name="StarLoan">
  <port name="LoanServicePort" binding="tns:LoanServiceBinding">
    <soap:address location="http://localhost:9700/orabpel/default/StarLoan"/>
  </port>
</service>

<service name="UnitedLoan">
  <port name="LoanServicePort" binding="tns:LoanServiceBinding">
    <soap:address location="http://localhost:9700/orabpel/default/UnitedLoan"/>
  </port>
</service>

<service name="AmericanLoan">
  <port name="LoanServicePort" binding="tns:LoanServiceBinding">
    <soap:address
location="http://localhost:9700/orabpel/default/AmericanLoan"/>
  </port>
</service>
```

It is important to understand that there is no "real" service called `LoanService`. Rather, `LoanService` is a template from which you select one of the real loan provider services (`UnitedLoan`, `AmericanLoan`, or `StarLoan`). This approach works as long as the real services all support the same interface (the same data types, messages, roles, ports, and partner link types) as that defined in the template WSDL. It is important to define this template interface carefully because a change here can affect many processes down the line.

The `LoanService.wsdl` file defines all the service options that the parent process can elect to call dynamically. This model requires a redeployment of the WSDL file as each new service is added. This approach represents a remarkable improvement over modifying the parent process to include new partner links and routing logic for each new service. (Later you will see how to disassociate the service endpoints from the WSDL file as well.)

Returning to the `DynamicPartnerlink.bpel` file, the next feature we want to look at is the `partnerReference` variable:

```
<variable name="partnerReference" element="wsa:EndpointReference"/>
```

This variable is of the type EndpointReference. It has a namespace wsa: defined at the top of the BPEL file as:

```
xmlns:wsa="http://schemas.xmlsoap.org/ws/2003/03/addressing"
```

The WS-Addressing standard provides the schema for the EndpointReference type. You can <assign> variables of this type to a partner link in order to modify the address and service information, thus providing the ability to modify the partner link at run time.

The DynamicPartnerLink process basically consists of a switch. It inspects the "provider" string passed in by the caller. Then, it assigns an EndpointReference XML data structure to the partnerReference variable containing the information relevant to the service that you're requesting. After the switch, the partnerReference variable is assigned to the LoanService partner link, and the partner link is invoked.

Here's how to accomplish this task when the input string (the service provider) is "united":

```
<assign>
 <copy>
  <from>
   <EndpointReference
           xmlns="http://schemas.xmlsoap.org/ws/2003/03/addressing">
   <Address>http://localhost:9700/orabpel/default/UnitedLoan</Address>
   <ServiceName
     xmlns:ns1="http://services.otn.com">ns1:UnitedLoan</ServiceName>
   </EndpointReference>
  </from>
  <to variable="partnerReference"/>
 </copy>
</assign>
```

Everything between the <from> and </from> tags is literal XML that you're assigning to the partnerReference variable. This data will override the address and service specified in the LoanService partner link when you assign the partnerReference variable to that link.

Now that you've explored the use of the LoanService partner link and LoanService.wsdl to invoke services selected at run time, you can move on to building a dynamic process.

Creating a Dynamic BPEL Process

Now, let's create a dynamic BPEL process from scratch.

1. **Create a new BPEL project**: Create a new asynchronous BPEL Process Project in JDeveloper and name it MyDL.

2. **Import the** LoanService.wsdl **file from the DynamicPartnerLink sample**: Copy the LoanService.wsdl file from the DynamicPartnerLink sample into the working directory of the MyDL project ([BPEL_HOME]\integration\jdev\jdev\mywork\ workspace1\MyDL by default). (This approach will save you the time and trouble of creating your own dynamic WSDL and sub-process services.) Then right-click the MyDL project in the Applications Navigator and select Add to Project.... Pick the LoanService.wsdl file from the directory and click OK.

The LoanService.wsdl file has not yet been added to the bpel.xml file. You won't do that until much later in the process when you implement the EndpointReference variable.

3. **Create the loan service partner link template**: Right-click one of the swim lanes and select Create Partner Link.... Fill in the dialog as shown in the screenshot below. To fill in the WSDL File location, use the Browse WSDL Files from Local File System button 🏷 (left of the flashlight) and select the LoanService.wsdl file from your MyDL project directory. Click on OK to create the partner link.

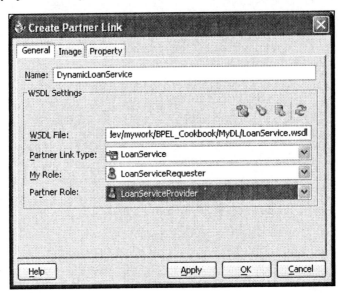

4. **Create the** invoke **and** receive **actions to call out to the DynamicLoanService partner link**: Drag one each of the invoke and receive actions from the component palette into your process (between the receiveInput and callbackClient actions). Drag one of the arrows from invoke to the DynamicLoanService partner link and create the input variable. Do the same for receive. Variables should be called loanInput and loanOutput.

5. **Configure input data** loanInput: Typically you would modify the MyDL.wsdl file to get the loan input data from the user. For the sake of simplicity here, you'll just hard-code an assign to populate the loanInput variable. Place the assign after the receiveInput action and create a copy rule that puts the value "123456789" (this is a string, not a number; so don't forget to quote it) into the SSN element of loanInput as follows:

```
<assign name="PopulateSSN">
 <copy>
  <from expression="'123456789'"/>
  <to variable="loanInput" part="payload"
query="/ns2:loanApplication/ns2:SSN"/>
 </copy>
</assign>
```

6. **Create the** `partnerReference` **variable**: In the Structure window, expand the Variables tree, followed by Process, and then select the Variables item.

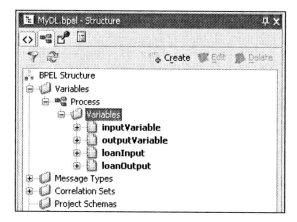

Right-click on Variables and select Create Variable.... Set the name of your variable to partnerReference and set the type to Element. Click on the flashlight icon next to the element box to bring up the type chooser. Find the type EndpointReference under Project WSDL Files | LoanService.wsdl | Inline Schemas | schema:

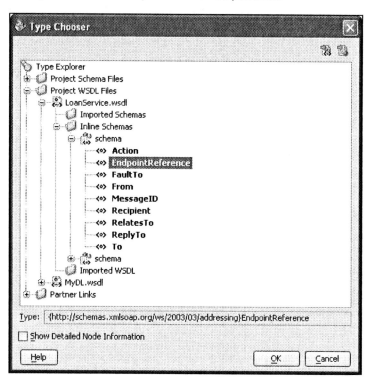

7. **Set up the** `partnerReference` **variable**: Create another `assign` before the DynamicLoanService invoke. Use this `assign` to set up the `partnerReference` variable. Initially you'll hard-code it to the `UnitedLoan` service, but you'll make it dynamic in the next section.

Here, you can avoid the issue encountered in the DynamicPartnerLink sample by reformatting the `EndpointReference` XML data. Create a copy rule that populates the `partnerReference` variable with this empty `EndpointReference`:

```
<EndpointReference xmlns="http://schemas.xmlsoap.org/ws/2003/03/addressing"
    xmlns:ns1="http://services.otn.com">
      <Address/>
      <ServiceName/>
</EndpointReference>
```

In the "from" block of the copy rule, be sure to select the type "XML Fragment" before entering the information above. You have to make this copy in order to establish the namespace information for the `partnerReference` because the `partnerReference` variable is treated as a separate XML document when it is copied over to the DynamicLoanService partner link. Otherwise, expect to get a null pointer exception when you try to assign the `partnerReference` variable to the partner link.

Now you can populate the `<ServiceName>` and `<Address>` elements of the `partnerReference` variable with standard copy rules. Be sure to specify the same namespace for the service (`ns1`) as what is defined in your blank endpoint reference. The `<assign>` should look like this:

```
<assign name="SetupPartnerlink">
  <copy>
    <from>
      <EndpointReference
          xmlns="http://schemas.xmlsoap.org/ws/2003/03/addressing"
          xmlns:ns1="http://services.otn.com">
        <Address/>
        <ServiceName/>
      </EndpointReference>
    </from>
    <to variable="partnerReference"/>
  </copy>
  <copy>
    <from expression="'ns1:UnitedLoan'"/>
    <to variable="partnerReference"
        query="/ns3:EndpointReference/ns3:ServiceName"/>
  </copy>
  <copy>
    <from expression="'http://localhost:9700/orabpel/default/UnitedLoan'"/>
    <to variable="partnerReference"
        query="/ns3:EndpointReference/ns3:Address"/>
  </copy>
</assign>
```

Also note that it is not until this point, when you use the `partnerReference` variable, that the `LoanService.wsdl` file is added to your `bpel.xml` file (so that the `EndpointReference` schema can be accessed).

8. **Copy the** `partnerReference` **variable into the DynamicLoanService partner link**: Create the new `assign` between the `SetupPartnerlink` action and the `invoke` for the DynamicLoanService. Create a new copy rule and set it up as shown below:

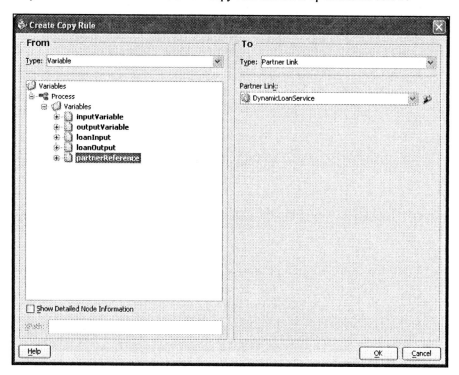

After these steps are completed, a dynamic BPEL process is created. The process has hard-coded address assignments. You can remedy this situation by replacing the last two copy rules in step 7 with information collected at run time. The BPEL Process diagram is shown in the following screenshot:

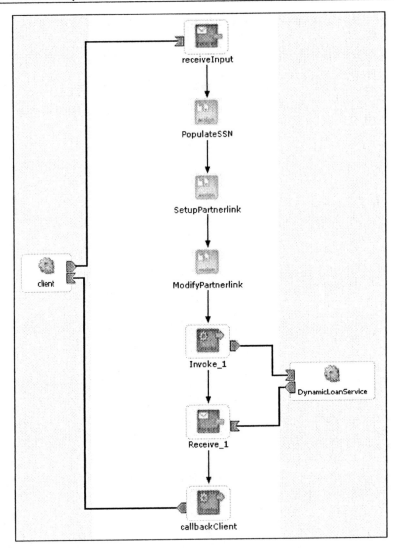

Increasing the Effectiveness of Dynamic Processes

As you've seen in the previous example, LoanService.wsdl lists all the possible services called dynamically at run time. You can enrich this dynamism of business process by eliminating the need to modify the business process every time a new service is added. New services are defined in WSDL and WSDL is re-deployed to make the new service available.

You could even take this dynamism one level higher: A WSDL-driven approach requires the knowledge of the location of new services at design time, but you can go one step further and make processes WSDL independent. This approach will eliminate the need to re-deploy the WSDL each time a service is added.

Eliminating Address Dependency at Run Time

Service addresses can change frequently, but you can shield dynamic processes from these changes at run time. If you assign only a service name and not an address, then the address for the service will be retrieved from the WSDL instead. To demonstrate, remove the stub for the address (`<Address/>`) from the XML fragment in the template copy rule. Make a backup copy of the MyDL.bpel file before you do so, as you will want the address information back shortly. Also remove the copy rule that manipulates the address from your SetupPartnerLink `<assign>` statement. The SetupPartnerlink `<assign>` should now look like this:

```
<assign name="SetupPartnerlink">
  <copy>
    <from>
      <EndpointReference
          xmlns="http://schemas.xmlsoap.org/ws/2003/03/addressing"
          xmlns:ns1="http://services.otn.com">
        <ServiceName/>
      </EndpointReference>
    </from>
    <to variable="partnerReference"/>
  </copy>
  <copy>
    <from expression="'ns1:UnitedLoan'"/>
    <to variable="partnerReference"
        query="/ns3:EndpointReference/ns3:ServiceName"/>
  </copy>
</assign>
```

Now, deploy and run the MyDL process again. Despite the lack of an address, it still makes a successful call to the UnitedLoan sub-process. This action can be verified by looking at the process tree view in the BPEL console. The result is that it is possible to modify the behavior of dynamic processes by simply deploying a new WSDL, which will contain modified address information for the service. The tradeoff is that in order to add new services, the WSDL will need to be modified and redeployed.

WSDL-Independent Services

In some cases, in addition to having many services to manage, you may also have a situation where the service addresses change frequently or where you want to avoid frequent updates to the WSDL file. Allowing the process to specify the address of the endpoint reference at run time can solve this problem.

Go back to the previous version of the MyDL.bpel file that has the address manipulation copy rules. Instead of removing the address information, remove the *service* information both from the template XML fragment and the ServiceName copy rule. The `<assign>` should now look like this:

```
<assign name="SetupPartnerlink">
  <copy>
    <from>
      <EndpointReference
          xmlns="http://schemas.xmlsoap.org/ws/2003/03/addressing"
          xmlns:ns1="http://services.otn.com">
        <Address/>
      </EndpointReference>
    </from>
    <to variable="partnerReference"/>
  </copy>
```

```
            <copy>
              <from expression="'http://localhost:9700/orabpel/default/UnitedLoan'"/>
              <to variable="partnerReference"
                   query="/ns3:EndpointReference/ns3:Address"/>
            </copy>
          </assign>
```

When you run the sample, the process makes the correct call to the UnitedLoan service, even though the service name is not specified. You can create the DynamicPartnerLink WSDL with only a single dummy service and call out to other services not listed in the WSDL as long as the addresses of those services is known at run time. If you don't specify an address for some reason, it will use the address of the default service in the WSDL. Therefore, it may be a good idea to have that service point to a real BPEL process, possibly one that logs an error or sends a notification.

One application of this technique is in building a framework for exception handling. If you have more than one available address where a given service is available (such as a local server and a remote redundant server), you can roll over to the secondary address when a call to the primary fails, by using an exception handler to override the address information in the endpoint reference and retry the invocation of the service.

Invoking Multiple Dynamic Processes

In some cases, a single data set may need to be passed to multiple sub-processes either in sequence or in parallel. You can use one or more while loops to implement this type of behavior.

Let's look at a quick example. A loan service provider's availability could be based on the day of the week. This information is stored in the database. A loan request arrives on Monday, and when the database is queried, it returns with a list of available Loan Service Providers (United and Star). To process the loan, the United and Star sub-processes will need to be called, either sequentially or in parallel. The database query returns the following result:

```
          <dbOutput>
            <part xmlns:xsi="http://www.w3.org/2001/XMLSchema-instance" name="response-
              headers">null</part>
            <part xmlns:xsi="http://www.w3.org/2001/XMLSchema-instance"
              name="DynamiclinksCollection">
            <n:DynamiclinksCollection
                xmlns:n=http://xmlns.oracle.com/pcbpel/adapter/db/top/MyDynamicLink
                xmlns:xsi="http://www.w3.org/2001/XMLSchema-instance">
             <Dynamiclinks>
              <address>http://localhost:9700/orabpel/default/UnitedLoan</address>
              <day>monday</day>
              <uid>1</uid>
             </Dynamiclinks>
             <Dynamiclinks>
              <address>http://localhost:9700/orabpel/default/StarLoan</address>
              <day>united</day>
              <uid>4</uid>
             </Dynamiclinks>
            </n:DynamiclinksCollection>
            </part>
          </dbOutput>
```

In order to call these in sequence, you would create a while loop. This while loop gets the address from the collection and performs a dynamic invoke/receive on each service.

```
<!-- first set up the counter variable "i" -->
<assign name="CounterReset">
  <copy>
    <from expression="1"/>
    <to variable="i"/>
  </copy>
</assign>

<!-- while loop goes until all link collection notes are done -->
<while name="LoanLoop" condition="bpws:getVariableData('i') <=
    count(bpws:getVariableData('dbOutput','DynamiclinksCollection',
    '/ns3:Dynamiclin ksCollection/Dynamiclinks'))">
  <sequence name="Sequence_1">

<!-- reset the endpoint with the usual xml fragment -->
    <assign name="ClearEndpoint">
      <copy>
        <from>
          <EndpointReference
            xmlns="http://schemas.xmlsoap.org/ws/2003/03/addressing"
            xmlns:ns1="http://services.otn.com">
            <Address/>
          </EndpointReference>
        </from>
        <to variable="partnerReference"/>
      </copy>
    </assign>

<!-- set the address in the endpoint variable
    based on the current node -->
    <assign name="SetEndpoint">
      <copy>
        <from variable="dbOutput" part="DynamiclinksCollection"
            query="/ns3:DynamiclinksCollection/Dynamiclinks
            [number(bpws:getVariableData('i'))]/address"/>
        <to variable="partnerReference"
            query="/wsa:EndpointReference/wsa:Address"/>
      </copy>
    </assign>

<!-- copy the endpoint variable into the partner link -->
    <assign name="DoPartnerlink">
      <copy>
        <from variable="partnerReference"/>
        <to partnerLink="LoanService"/>
      </copy>
    </assign>
<!-- invoke the partner link -->
    <invoke name="Invoke_2" partnerLink="LoanService"
        portType="ns2:LoanService" operation="initiate"
        inputVariable="loanInput"/>

<!-- be sure to increment your counter or you have an infinite loop -->
    <assign name="CounterIncrement">
      <copy>
        <from expression="bpws:getVariableData('i')+1"/>
        <to variable="i"/>
      </copy>
    </assign>
  </sequence>
</while>
```

In this example you're calling asynchronous services. It is possible to call them in parallel by removing the `<receive>` from the `<invoke>` while loop and giving it a while loop of its own. Responses from each of the callout processes will queue up until a `<receive>` is run to catch them. The receive task will collect the responses in the order that they return. This approach will prevent a response from a short-running task from being queued up behind the response from a long-running task.

It is not recommended to proceed out of the `<receive>` while loop until all of asynchronous responses have been collected.

Conclusion

As you've seen here, by binding dynamically using endpoint referencing, BPEL processes can become more agile and can adapt to changing business conditions quickly. By decoupling business logic from partner addressing, you can make processes much more adaptive and portable.

8

Using WSIF for Integration

by Matjaž B. Jurič

Learn how BPEL processes can access Java classes and EJBs using WSIF.

In real-world scenarios, a BPEL business process will often have to connect to an existing application or system. Of particular interest here is connectivity to J2EE artifacts, such as Java classes, Enterprise Java Beans (EJBs), Java Message Service (JMS), ERP systems accessible through Java Connector Architecture (JCA), JDBC databases, or other Java resources.

It is possible to convert these resources to a web service, but that approach has several disadvantages:

- The performance overhead of invoking web service operations is several orders of magnitude larger than that of invoking native Java classes, and an order of magnitude larger than that of invoking EJBs or other native Java resources. (See the tip box that follows overleaf.)

- Web services invocations lack the important capability to propagate contexts during transactions. In contrast, when using Java resources directly, transaction context can be propagated automatically if the Java resource provides such support (as EJB and JCA do, for example).

Hence, the better approach is to access these external resources natively. Native connectivity to Java resources is not a standard feature of BPEL, but Oracle BPEL Process Manager offers a solution for this purpose—**Web Services Invocation Framework** (WSIF) at http://ws.apache.org/wsif/— that does not require modifications or extensions to BPEL code. This capability greatly extends the reach of BPEL and makes it suitable for enterprise application integration (EAI).

In this chapter of *The BPEL Cookbook*, you will learn how BPEL processes can access resources other than web services using WSIF.

Performance and Transactional Differences between SOAP and WSIF Bindings

Invoking Java resources is usually faster than invoking web services. Particularly when using plain Java classes, the performance of method invocations is several orders of magnitude better. Java classes are loaded in the application server process and BPEL processes can access their methods directly.

When using EJBs, you in general have the choice of using local or remote interfaces. Local interfaces are almost as fast as plain Java classes. The difference arises from the fact that there is a certain overhead of the EJB container. If on the other hand you use remote EJB interfaces, then the performance penalty is larger (but according to my measurements still lower than with web services, as I will explain shortly).

EJB remote interfaces are accessed through RMI-IIOP, which requires a stub on the client side and uses the skeleton on the server side. The remote method invocation has to pass several layers before it reaches the EJB, which takes time. Therefore, when using remote interfaces, you should use coarse-grained methods and become familiar with other J2EE patterns that influence performance. Also keep in mind that some application servers optimize the communication with EJBs if they are deployed within the same application server.

With web services, the situation from the performance perspective is even more complicated. In general the communication with web services is comparable to that with remote interfaces of EJBs. In contrast to EJBs, web services use SOAP, which is less efficient than binary IIOP. Thus, more processing overhead related to constructing and parsing of SOAP messages and XML serialization is required on the caller and receiver sides. My tests have revealed that invoking a web service is about five to nine times slower than invoking a session bean.

Using WSIF to invoke Java resources also provides advantages with transactions. Java resources, such as EJBs and JCA, support transactions through JTA, which makes use of JTS. JTS is based on CORBA Object Transaction Service, which provides support for distributed transactions based on the X/Open DTP standard. Java resources that support transactions through JTA (EJBs, JCA, etc.) can participate in distributed transactions using the **2PC (Two-Phase Commit)** protocol.

WSIF supports automatic propagation of transactional context between involved Java resources using the XA interface (automatically exposed by JTS). This means that if you used several transaction-aware resources from your BPEL process through WSIF (two EJBs for example), the transaction context would be automatically propagated between resources. Should an exception occur, the whole transaction would roll back automatically without the need to define a compensation handler in the BPEL process.

Without WSIF-enabled Java resources—or if using web services only, or first converting Java resources to web services—you could not take advantage of this feature. Rather, you would have to manually define compensation handlers for each web service. This is very important for mission-critical processes and simplifies their design and development.

Understanding WSIF

Consider a business process for buying books. This asynchronous process has three web services: a Book Rating web service, which returns the rating of a specific book ranging from 0 to 5 (best), and one web service each for two identical Book Store services, which return the book price. The process selects the lower price and makes the book purchase. In this example, fault handlers are defined and the process is divided into scopes (check 1_BuyBook\BuyBook.bpel).

Assume that to obtain a book rating you would prefer to use a Java class, EJB (session bean), service from an enterprise information system that can be accessed through JCA, or a similar Java resource. To incorporate such resources (and possibly any other resources for which bindings exist) into BPEL processes using Oracle BPEL Process Manager, you need only modify the service binding (WSDL), not the BPEL process itself. Thus to replace the Book Rating web service with a Java class, you only have to modify the WSDL of the web service (more on that later).

WSIF, an Apache technology originally developed by IBM alphaWorks as a part of its web services toolkit, is the underlying technology that makes this approach possible. It extends the web services model by allowing you to describe services in WSDL, even if it's not a web service that communicates through SOAP. WSIF also allows you to map such a service to the actual implementation and protocol.

In other words, you can bind the abstract description of any partner web service used in the BPEL process to a corresponding resource, which can communicate using one of the supported WSIF bindings. The WSIF used by Oracle BPEL Process Manager 10.1.2 supports Java classes, EJB, JCA, HTTP GET and POST, and sockets; you can also define custom WSIF bindings and use practically any resource from BPEL.

This approach makes BPEL very useful for EAI as well as B2B. Enterprise information systems usually consist of many different software pieces, such as legacy applications accessible though JCA, EJBs, web services developed on different platforms, and so on. To integrate all these pieces you have to deal with different protocols. For example, if software migrates to a different server or has been upgraded to use a new technology, you have to upgrade the integration code—unless you use WSIF.

WSIF offers other important benefits:

- Invoking services through WSIF maintains the performance of native protocols. Thus, when invoking Java resources, native Java classes, EJBs, or any other resources, you do not have to pay the performance penalty of web services.

- WSIF enables automatic propagation of transactional contexts between invoked transaction-aware Java resources using Java Transaction API (JTA). That way Java resources can participate in distributed transactions.

To learn how WSIF works, here you'll modify our BPEL process for buying books and invoke a Java class and then an EJB. Remember that with WSIF you will only have to modify the WSDL of the service, not the BPEL code. Through the modifications in WSDL, you will bind the call to the Java resource instead of a web service.

First, we'll focus on using a Java class instead of the Book Rating web service. To replace the web service, you need to have a Java class with exactly the same interface as the web service; this will require development of a Java class based on the WSDL contract. The other possibility would be to adapt the WSDL to an existing Java class (or another resource, let's say EJB). The first approach is better, because it is a so-called contract-first approach. This way the interface of the service is adapted to the needs of the BPEL process and not vice versa.

Java-to-XML Bindings

To invoke a Java resource from BPEL, you will need to use data from BPEL variables, which are sent as input parameters to Java resources, and to send data from Java back to BPEL. BPEL variables are XML, whereas Java variables are not; therefore, you need a mapping between XML and Java.

To handle XML data from Java you have several options:

- **Handle XML manually through the DOM (Document Object Model) API**: This way the input and output parameters of the corresponding Java methods are of type Element from the W3C DOM API for Java. Use DOM methods to manipulate XML directly.

- **Use automated Java-to-XML bindings**: Java-to-XML binding enables automatic conversion of XML Schema types to Java types. To achieve this, interfaces and a set of Java classes are generated through which you manipulate the XML. This way XML is hidden and you can use it through interfaces (such as JavaBeans). Here you have two options:
    - Oracle BPEL Process Manager: Supports default Java-to-XML bindings through the use of XML façades.
    - Use of custom Java serializers: Oracle already provides custom serializers that support JAXB (Java API for XML Bindings), XML beans, and Axis beans. You can also write your own serializers (more about that later).

Let's have a look at the XML façades first.

XML Façades

XML façades are Oracle BPEL Process Manager's original Java-to-XML binding for WSIF and are an integral part of the product. XML façades are a set of Java interfaces and classes through which you can access and modify XML data stored in BPEL variables in a relatively easy way using get/set methods. In this manner you are not required to manipulate XML directly. Furthermore, the XML is hidden behind the façade and you can manipulate the data through regular Java interfaces, a concept known as XML serialization. The idea behind XML façades is to provide support for basic data types through mapping to built-in types and to generate Java classes from XML Schemas for complex types.

The automatic mapping for the basic data types between XML Schema and Java types is shown here:

XML Schema Type	Java Types
xs:string	· java.lang.String · char · java.lang.Character
xs:int, xs:integer	· int · java.lang.Integer · java.math.BigInteger
xs:long	· long · java.lang.Long
xs:short	· short · java.lang.Short
xs:float	· float · java.lang.Float
xs:double	· double · java.lang.Double · java.math.BigDecimal
xs:byte	· byte · java.lang.Byte
xs:Boolean	· boolean · java.lang.Boolean
dateTime	java.util.Calendar
date	java.util.Date

As you can see, most of the simple types can be mapped to either primitive or object types. This is useful as you can adapt the mapping to the actual types used in you Java code. In addition to simple types, you also need a way to map complex types, whether those defined in the <types> section of the WSDL or in the external XML Schema (XSD) files. For example, in your Book Rating web service WSDL, you'll notice an operation that takes input the BookRatingRequestMessage, which is of type BookDscType. The BookDscType complex XML type is used for the BookRatingRequestMessage and for the corresponding BookRatingRequest BPEL variable:

```
<xs:schema elementFormDefault="qualified"
           targetNamespace="http://oracle.com/service/bookrating/">

    <xs:complexType name="BookDscType">
      <xs:sequence>
        <xs:element name="Title" type="xs:string" />
        <xs:element name="ISSN" type="xs:string" />
        <xs:element name="Publisher" type="xs:string" />
        <xs:element name="Authors" type="xs:string" />
      </xs:sequence>
    </xs:complexType>

</xs:schema>
```

The XML façade for this complex XML type provides an interface and a class through which you can access the elements (title, ISSN, publisher, authors) using Java getter methods. The XML façade also allows you to modify the element data using setter methods.

An XML façade for this variable consists of an interface (IBookDscType), and a class (BookDscType) that provides the following methods:

- getTitle() and setTitle()
- getISSN() and setISSN()
- getPublisher() and setPublisher()
- getAuthors() and setAuthors()

There is also a factory class (BookDscTypeFactory) through which you can create the IBookDscType using the createFacade() method. XML façade makes the code simpler and easier to maintain; this is particularly true for larger variables with many member fields.

Oracle BPEL Process Manager provides a schema compiler utility called schemac. Using this utility you can generate XML façades. To generate the XML façade for BookRating.wsdl, use the following command line:

```
Z:\WSIF\2_JavaBindingClass>schemac BookRating.wsdl
-------------------------------------------------
Oracle XML Schema Processor Version 10.1.2.0.0
http://otn.oracle.com/bpel
Copyright (c) 2002-2004 - Oracle
(type schemac -help for help)
-------------------------------------------------

schemac> parsing schema file 'BookRating.wsdl' ...
schemac> Loaded schemas from wsdl located at BookRating.wsdl
schemac> generating XML business document ...
schemac> compiling XML business documents ...
Schemac completed successfully.

Z:\WSIF\2_JavaBindingClass>
```

To use these classes from Java resources, you will need to compile them into the c:\OraBPELPM_1\ integration\orabpel\system\classes directory where the BPEL server can access them.

The schemac utility has several options. You can use the -d switch to define the directory where the generated façade classes should be stored. To see the façade source code use the -trace option. The schemac utility can also be used to generate XML Schemas out of Java classes. This is useful if you would like to adapt the service interface to an existing Java resource. You have to use the -R switch and provide the Java class name without the extension.

Developing the Java Class

To replace the Book Rating web service with a Java class without modifying BPEL, you need a Java class that has the same interface (contract) as the original Book Rating web services. This means that the Java class has to provide the operations with the identical functionality, and that operations have to accept the same parameters and return the same result type—but the operation name needn't be identical.

Looking at the original WSDL, you'll see that the Book Rating web service provides an operation called BookRating, which takes an input and an output message and is thus synchronous:

```
<portType name="BookRatingPT">
  <operation name="BookRating">
    <input message="tns:BookRatingRequestMessage" />
    <output message="tns:BookRatingResponseMessage" />
  </operation>
</portType>
```

The signatures of both messages are as follows:

```
<message name="BookRatingRequestMessage">
  <part name="book" type="tns:BookDscType" />
</message>

<message name="BookRatingResponseMessage">
  <part name="rating" type="xs:int" />
</message>
```

The input parameter to the operation is of type BookDscType. To map the BookDscType to Java, use the corresponding XML façade, which you generated earlier using the schemac tool. The return type of the operation is the BookRatingResponseMessage message, which is of type xs:int. xs:int type maps to java.lang.Integer. (It could also map to int or java.math.BigInteger, but you are using java.lang.Integer here.)

You are now ready to write the Java equivalent class for the Book Rating web service. Call the new Java class BookRatingJava, which will have a single method called getBookRating. The method body will be oversimplified—you will print a notification to the server console and return the rating of 4. (In a real-world example, you could calculate the rating based on data in the database, for example.) The code is as follows (note how you can access the book title and ISSN using getTitle() and getISSN() methods respectively):

```
package com.oracle.rating;
import com.oracle.service.bookrating.*;

public class BookRatingJava {

  public Integer getBookRating (BookDscType book) {
    System.out.println("Book rating for "+book.getTitle()+
("+book.getISSN()+"): 4.");
    return new Integer(4);
  }

}
```

The console output is added here to verify that the process really calls the Java class and not the web service.

Defining WSIF Bindings in WSDL

To "persuade" the BPEL process to use the Java class instead of the web service, you have to define the WSIF bindings to the Java class. This is done in the Book Rating WSDL, where you add the binding section.

Each WSIF binding consists of two parts. First, you have to define the actual binding, where you specify:

- Type of binding used (Java class, EJB, JCA, and so on).

- Mapping of types, where you specify the mapping of XML types to the destination types (for Java resources these are Java types). You have to define the mapping for all complex types; simple types are mapped automatically based on the table presented earlier.

- Mapping of operations, where you have to specify for each WSDL operation (defined under the <portType> tag) the corresponding operation in the destination resource (for example, the name of the method of a Java class).

Second, you have to specify the service you will be using. Here you specify the exact name of the resource. If it is a Java class, specify its full name (including the package name).

In a real-world scenario, you may have a resource, such as a Java class or an EJB, for which a WSDL will not exist. Then you have to go through the following steps:

1. Define the Java-to-XML bindings, where you select how to map input parameters and return value to XML. You can use XML façades and simplify the work using the schemac tool with the -R switch, which will generate an XML Schema based on a Java class.

2. Define the signature for each operation and the corresponding input and output messages. Later in this chapter (in the *Exception Handling* section), you will also see how to handle faults.

3. Add the WSIF binding.

4. Add the <partnerLinkType> declaration in order to use the WSDL from the BPEL process.

Particularly in the first two steps you can use a tool or a wizard for automatic conversion of resources to web services. Such tools are available for most environments. Of course you do not actually convert the resource to a web service, but can make use of the generated WSDL (with additional modifications).

WSIF Binding for Java Class

Let's now define the WSIF binding for BookRatingJava class. Start by defining the two namespaces used by WSIF providers in the root element of the WSDL document, the <definitions> tag. The format namespace is used to define the type mappings and the java namespace to define the operation mappings and the full name of the Java class:

```
<?xml version="1.0" encoding="utf-8" ?>
<definitions xmlns:xs="http://www.w3.org/2001/XMLSchema"
             xmlns:tns="http://oracle.com/service/bookrating/"
             targetNamespace="http://oracle.com/service/bookrating/"
             xmlns="http://schemas.xmlsoap.org/wsdl/"
             xmlns:plnk="http://schemas.xmlsoap.org/ws/2003/05/partner-link/"
             xmlns:format="http://schemas.xmlsoap.org/wsdl/formatbinding/"
             xmlns:java="http://schemas.xmlsoap.org/wsdl/java/" >
    ...
```

Next, add the binding section. This section is usually located after port type declarations and before partner link types. Here you define a Java binding for the BookRatingPT port type:

1. Define the type mapping from XML to Java. The input parameter XML type BookDscType is mapped to the com.oracle.service.bookrating.BookDscType Java class. Please note that you do not have to provide the mapping for output XML xs:int type, because it maps automatically to java.lang.Integer.

2. Also define that the WSDL operation BookRating is mapped to the Java method getBookRating(). Please note that the name of the WSDL operation and the method name of the Java class do not need to be equal, but the types of input and return parameters do:

```
...
    <binding name="JavaBinding" type="tns:BookRatingPT">

        <java:binding/>

        <format:typeMapping encoding="Java" style="Java">
          <format:typeMap typeName="tns:BookDscType"
                     formatType="com.oracle.service.bookrating.BookDscType" />
        </format:typeMapping>

        <operation name="BookRating">
          <java:operation methodName="getBookRating"/>
          <input/>
          <output/>
        </operation>

    </binding>
...
```

Next, specify the service used. Define that the service is provided by the Java class. The Book Rating service will use the com.oracle.rating.BookRatingJava Java class:

```
...
    <service name="BookRating">

        <port name="JavaPort" binding="tns:JavaBinding">
          <java:address className="com.oracle.rating.BookRatingJava"/>
        </port>

    </service>
```

The rest of the Book Rating WSDL (including partner link types) has not changed.

Testing the Example

You are almost ready to test the example and verify that the BPEL process will use the Java class instead of the original web service. Remember, you have modified the WSDL only; you have not made any changes to the BPEL process code.

You will use the original BPEL code and the same partner link and invoke the BookRatingJava Java class with the usual <invoke> activity used for invoking the web service. Recall the BPEL code for the invocation of the Book Rating service:

```
<!-- Synchronously invoke the Book Rating Web Service -->
<scope name="BookRatingInvoke">

    <faultHandlers>

        <catchAll>
          <!-- If book rating is not available assign 0 -->
          <assign>
            <copy>
              <from expression="number(0)"/>
              <to variable="BookRatingResponse" part="rating"/>
            </copy>
          </assign>
        </catchAll>

    </faultHandlers>

    <invoke partnerLink="BookRating"
            portType="bkr:BookRatingPT"
            operation="BookRating"
            inputVariable="BookRatingRequest"
            outputVariable="BookRatingResponse" />

</scope>
```

Before we can test the example we have to do a few "book-keeping" activities. First, we have to ensure that the BPEL process will use the modified WSDL. To achieve this, modify the bpel.xml file and specify that the BookRating.wsdl file should be taken from the current directory and not from the web service itself:

```
<?xml version="1.0" encoding="UTF-8"?>
<BPELSuitcase>
  <BPELProcess src="BuyBook.bpel" id="BuyBookJavaBinding">
    <partnerLinkBindings>
      <partnerLinkBinding name="Client">
        <property name="wsdlLocation">
          BuyBook.wsdl
        </property>
      </partnerLinkBinding>
      <partnerLinkBinding name="BookRating">
        <property name="wsdlLocation">
          BookRating.wsdl
        </property>
      </partnerLinkBinding>
      <partnerLinkBinding name="BookStore1">
        <property name="wsdlLocation">
          http://localhost:9700/orabpel/default/BookStore1/BookStore1?wsdl
        </property>
      </partnerLinkBinding>
      <partnerLinkBinding name="BookStore2">
        <property name="wsdlLocation">
          http://localhost:9700/orabpel/default/BookStore2/BookStore2?wsdl
        </property>
      </partnerLinkBinding>
    </partnerLinkBindings>
  </BPELProcess>
</BPELSuitcase>
```

We then generate the XML façade using the schemac utility and compile the BookRatingJava class. You have to deploy the XML façade and the Java class to the c:\OraBPELPM_1\integration\ bpelpm\orabpel\system\classes directory, where the BPEL server can locate and use them. The easiest way is to modify the build.xml, which should invoke the schemac compiler, the javac compiler, and the bpelc compiler:

```
<?xml version="1.0"?>
<project name="BuyBookJavaBinding" default="all" basedir=".">
  <property name="deploy" value="default"/>
  <property name="rev" value="1.0"/>

   <target name="CompileJava">
     <schemac input="${basedir}/BookRating.wsdl"
              out="${home}/system/classes"/>
     <javac srcdir="${basedir}/src" destdir="${home}/system/classes"/>
   </target>

   <target name="main">
     <bpelc home="${home}" rev="${rev}" deploy="${deploy}"/>
   </target>

   <target name="all" depends="CompileJava, main"/>

</project>
```

After starting the obant utility, you should get the following output:

```
Z:\WSIF\2_JavaBindingClass>obant

Z:\WSIF\2_JavaBindingClass>SETLOCAL
Buildfile: build.xml

CompileJava:
  [schemac] schemac> parsing schema file
'Z:\WSIF\2_JavaBindingClass/BookRating.
wsdl' ...
  [schemac] schemac> Loaded schemas from wsdl located at
Z:\WSIF\2_JavaBindingCl
ass/BookRating.wsdl
  [schemac] schemac> generating XML business document ...
  [schemac] schemac> compiling XML business documents ...
    [javac] Compiling 1 source file to C:\OraBPELPM_1\integration\orabpel\
system\classes

main:
    [bpelc] validating "Z:\WSIF\2_JavaBindingClass\BuyBook.bpel" ...
    [bpelc] BPEL suitcase deployed to:
C:\OraBPELPM_1\integration\orabpel\domain
s\default\deploy

all:

BUILD SUCCESSFUL
Total time: 17 seconds

Z:\WSIF\2_JavaBindingClass>ENDLOCAL

Z:\WSIF\2_JavaBindingClass>
```

Next, use the BPEL Console to start the process. In the visual flow window, you can observe the execution of the process. Note that the <invoke> activity has been used in BPEL and that the book rating is 4, in contrast to the original Book Rating web services, which returned 5:

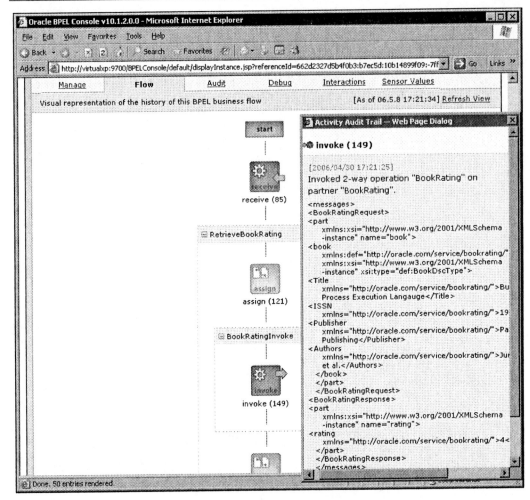

To be absolutely sure that the BPEL Process Manager has invoked the Java class, the BPEL Process Manager console window will show the following output:

```
05/10/19 19:35:36 Book rating for Business Process Execution Language
(1-904811-18-3): 4.
```

Exception Handling

When invoking Java resources from BPEL we need a way to propagate Java exceptions to BPEL. With WSIF, we can map Java exceptions to WSDL faults and handle them using BPEL fault handlers. The exception serializer is responsible for the mapping. Oracle BPEL Process Manager provides a default exception serializer; alternatively, you can write our own custom serializer.

To demonstrate how Java exceptions can be propagated to BPEL, we will extend our example. First, we use the default serializer, and then extend the example with a custom serializer. We need to take the following steps:

1. Define a user exception in Java.
2. Modify the BookRatingJava Java class to throw the exception.
3. Define the corresponding fault in the WSDL. This includes the definition of XML Schema type for the fault message, the fault message, and addition of the <fault> message to the WSDL <operation> description.
4. Define the WSIF binding for the exception.

Define User Exception in Java

First, define a user exception for signaling that a book, for which the rating has been acquired, does not exist. You will name the exception BookDoesNotExistException. The following code shows the exception in Java:

```
package com.oracle.rating;

public class BookDoesNotExistException extends Exception
{
   String detailDesc;
   String bookTitle;

   public BookDoesNotExistException(String message, String detailDesc,
                                    String bookTitle)
   {
     super(message);
     this.detailDesc = detailDesc;
     this.bookTitle = bookTitle;
   }

   public String getDetailDesc()
   {
     return detailDesc;
   }

   public String getBookTitle()
   {
     return bookTitle;
   }
}
```

Throw Java Exception

Next, modify the BookRatingJava Java class. You will throw the exception if the ISSN of the book equals 999:

```
package com.oracle.rating;

import com.oracle.service.bookrating.*;

public class BookRatingJavaUserException {

   public Integer getBookRating (BookDscType book) throws
BookDoesNotExistException {

      if (book.getISSN().equals("999"))
         throw(new BookDoesNotExistException("Book does not exist",
                                 "Book (ISSN="+book.getISSN()+") does not exist",
                                 book.getTitle()));
```

125

```
        System.out.println("Book rating for "+book.getTitle()+
                                " ("+book.getISSN()+"): 4.");

        return new Integer(4);

    }
}
```

Define Fault in WSDL

In the next step, you will define the corresponding fault in WSDL. The Java exception will be propagated to this fault. As you will use the default exception serializer, you have to use a specific complex type that has two elements: faultstring and detail. Add this complex type to the <types> section of the Book Rating WSDL:

```
<xs:complexType name="BookDoesNotExistExceptionType">
  <xs:sequence>
    <xs:element name="faultstring" type="xs:string" />
    <xs:element name="detail" type="xs:string" />
  </xs:sequence>
</xs:complexType>
```

Next, define the corresponding message:

```
<message name="BookDoesNotExistException">
  <part name="exception" type="tns:BookDoesNotExistExceptionType" />
</message>
```

Finally, add the fault message to the BookRating operation signature:

```
<portType name="BookRatingPT">
  <operation name="BookRating">
    <input message="tns:BookRatingRequestMessage" />
    <output message="tns:BookRatingResponseMessage" />
    <fault name="BookDoesNotExistException" message="tns:BookDoesNotExistException" />
  </operation>
</portType>
```

The default exception serializer will create the fault element and fill the faultstring element with the content returned by Exception.getMessage() and the detail element with the content returned by Exception.toString().

Define WSIF Binding for Exception

Now you are ready to add the exception to the WSIF binding. You have to define the type mapping for the BookDoesNotExistExceptionType XML type, which in our case will map to the corresponding Java exception class—to the com.oracle.rating.BookDoesNotExistException. You also have to add the fault message name (BookDoesNotExistException) to the operation mapping part:

```
<binding name="JavaBinding" type="tns:BookRatingPT">
  <java:binding/>
  <format:typeMapping encoding="Java" style="Java">
    <format:typeMap typeName="tns:BookDscType"
                    formatType="com.oracle.service.bookrating.BookDscType" />
    <format:typeMap typeName="tns:BookDoesNotExistExceptionType"
```

```
                    formatType="com.oracle.rating.BookDoesNotExistException" />
    </format:typeMapping>
    <operation name="BookRating">
      <java:operation methodName="getBookRating"/>
      <input/>
      <output/>
      <fault name="BookDoesNotExistException"/>
    </operation>
  </binding>
```

For this example to work, you have to compile Java classes and deploy them to the
C:\OraBPELPM_1\integration\orabpel\system\classes directory, where the BPEL server can
access them. The easiest way is to use the obant utility with the example:

```
Z:\WSIF\3_JavaBindingUserExceptionDefaultSerializer>obant

Z:\WSIF\3_JavaBindingUserExceptionDefaultSerializer>SETLOCAL
Buildfile: build.xml

CompileJava:
  [schemac] schemac> parsing schema file
'Z:\WSIF\3_JavaBindingUserExceptionDefa
ultSerializer/BookRating.wsdl' ...
  [schemac] schemac> Loaded schemas from wsdl located at
Z:\WSIF\3_JavaBindingUs
erExceptionDefaultSerializer/BookRating.wsdl
  [schemac] schemac> generating XML business document ...
  [schemac] schemac> compiling XML business documents ...
    [javac] Compiling 2 source files to C:\OraBPELPM_1\in
tegration\orabpel\system\classes

main:
    [bpelc] validating
"Z:\WSIF\3_JavaBindingUserExceptionDefaultSerializer\BuyB
ook.bpel" ...
    [bpelc] BPEL suitcase deployed to:
C:\OraBPELPM_1\integration\orabpel\domain
s\default\deploy

all:

BUILD SUCCESSFUL
Total time: 18 seconds

Z:\WSIF\3_JavaBindingUserExceptionDefaultSerializer>ENDLOCAL

Z:\WSIF\3_JavaBindingUserExceptionDefaultSerializer>
```

After starting the example from the BPEL console and entering an ISSN of 999, you get the following output:

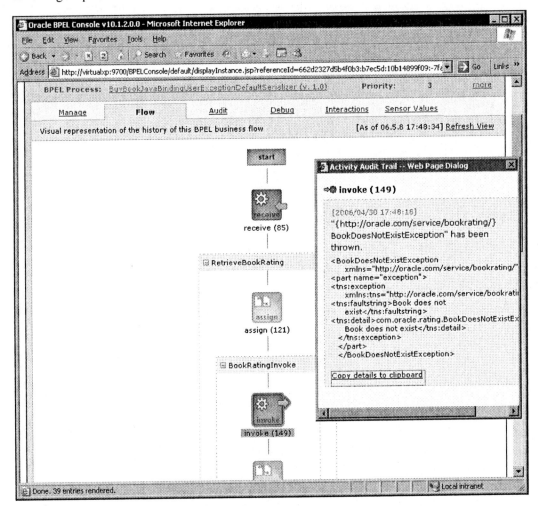

Custom Exception Serializers

If you are not happy with the structure of the WSDL fault (which consists of the faultstring and detail elements) and would prefer to have more control over the mapping of Java exceptions to WSDL faults, you can use custom exception serializers. A custom exception serializer is a Java class that maps the exception and its attributes to the complex type used for the WSDL fault. To see how custom serializer is developed, go through the following steps:

1. Define a custom complex type used for the WSDL fault message.
2. Write a custom exception serializer to propagate the Java exception to the WSDL fault.
3. Register the custom exception serializer.

First, define the XML Schema custom complex type to represent the Java exception that will include all three exception attributes, message, detail description, and book title. You will replace the default complex type with this type in the <types> section of the Book Rating WSDL:

```
<xs:complexType name="BookDoesNotExistExceptionType">
  <xs:sequence>
    <xs:element name="message" type="xs:string" />
    <xs:element name="detailDesc" type="xs:string" />
    <xs:element name="bookTitle" type="xs:string" />
  </xs:sequence>
</xs:complexType>
```

The custom exception serializer is a Java class that defines how the Java exception maps to the WSDL fault complex type. The exception serializer has to map the Java exception attributes to the corresponding XML elements of the fault message, and has to implement the following interface:

```
public interface IExceptionSerializer {

    public Element serialize(Throwable ex,
                             String messageName,
                             String namespaceURI);
}
```

For our example, we will name the custom exception serializer BookDoesNotExistExceptionSerializer and extend the existing ExceptionSerializer class. Using the DOM API, we will map the three attributes of the Java exception (message, detail description, and book title) to the earlier XML Schema type (BookDoesNotExistExceptionType):

```
package com.oracle.rating;

import org.w3c.dom.Element;

import com.collaxa.xml.XMLHelper;
import com.oracle.bpel.xml.util.ExceptionSerializer;
import com.oracle.bpel.xml.util.IExceptionSerializer;

public class BookDoesNotExistExceptionSerializer extends ExceptionSerializer
    implements IExceptionSerializer {

  public Element serialize(Throwable ex, String messageName,
                                         String namespaceURI) {

    if(ex instanceof BookDoesNotExistException)
    {
      BookDoesNotExistException brEx = (BookDoesNotExistException)ex;

      Element exceptionElement =
            XMLHelper.createRootElement(messageName, namespaceURI,"tns");

      Element messageElement =
            XMLHelper.createElement("message","tns",namespaceURI);
      messageElement.setNodeValue(brEx.getMessage());
      exceptionElement.appendChild(messageElement);

      Element detailElement =
            XMLHelper.createElement("detailDesc","tns",namespaceURI);
      detailElement.setNodeValue(brEx.getDetailDesc());
      exceptionElement.appendChild(detailElement);

      Element bookElement =
            XMLHelper.createElement("bookTitle","tns",namespaceURI);
      bookElement.setNodeValue(brEx.getBookTitle());
```

```
        exceptionElement.appendChild(bookElement);

        return exceptionElement;

    }
      return super.serialize(ex, messageName, namespaceURI);
    }

  }
```

The final step is to register the custom exception serializer with the Oracle BPEL Process Manager. This step will instruct the BPEL Process Manager to use your custom serializer instead of the default serializer. To do so, define the exceptionSerializer property in the bpel.xml deployment descriptor:

```
<partnerLinkBinding name="BookRating">
  <property name="wsdlLocation">
      BookRating.wsdl
  </property>
  <property name="exceptionSerializer">
      com.oracle.rating.BookDoesNotExistExceptionSerializer
  </property>
</partnerLinkBinding>
```

As with the previous example, you have to compile Java classes and deploy them to the C:\OraBPELPM_1\integration\orabpel\system\classes directory. Use the obant utility:

```
Z:\WSIF\3_JavaBindingUserExceptionCustomSerializer>obant

Z:\WSIF\3_JavaBindingUserExceptionCustomSerializer>SETLOCAL
Buildfile: build.xml

CompileJava:
   [schemac] schemac> parsing schema file
'Z:\WSIF\3_JavaBindingUserExceptionCust
omSerializer/BookRating.wsdl' ...
   [schemac] schemac> Loaded schemas from wsdl located at
Z:\WSIF\3_JavaBindingUS
erExceptionCustomSerializer/BookRating.wsdl
   [schemac] schemac> generating XML business document ...
   [schemac] schemac> compiling XML business documents ...
     [javac] Compiling 3 source files to
C:\OraBPELPM_1\integration\orabpel\system\classes

main:
     [bpelc] validating
"Z:\WSIF\3_JavaBindingUserExceptionCustomSerializer\BuyBo
ok.bpel" ...
     [bpelc] BPEL suitcase deployed to:
C:\OraBPELPM_1\integration\orabpel\domains\default\deploy

all:

BUILD SUCCESSFUL
Total time: 21 seconds

Z:\WSIF\3_JavaBindingUserExceptionCustomSerializer>ENDLOCAL

Z:\WSIF\3_JavaBindingUserExceptionCustomSerializer>
```

After starting the example from the BPEL console and entering an ISSN of 999, you'll get the following output. Notice the different fault structure.

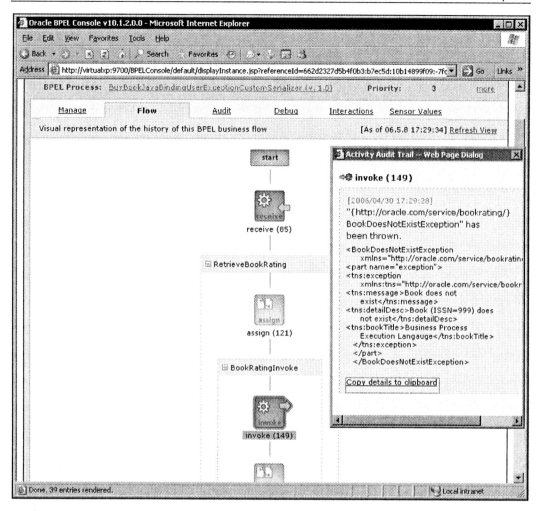

Custom Java Serializers

A custom Java serializer is a class that implements the IJavaSerializer interface. It has to provide the implementation of two methods: serialize() and deserialize().

```
public interface IJavaSerializer {

    public Element serialize(Object obj, Class type, String name,
                             String namespaceURI,
                             String prefix, Map classMap) throws Exception;
    public Object deserialize(Element el, Class type) throws Exception;
}
```

Similar to custom exception serializers, you have to deploy the compiled class to the c:\OraBPELPM_1\ integration\orabpel\system\classes directory and define the javaSerializer property in the bpel.xml deployment descriptor:

```
<partnerLinkBinding name="helper">
    <property name="wsdlLocation">HelperService.wsdl</property>
    <property name="javaSerializer">
      com.oracle.bpel.xml.util.MyCustomSerializer
    </property>
</partnerLinkBinding>
```

Oracle provides three custom serializers out of the box: for Java API for XML Bindings (JAXB), XML beans, and Axis beans.

JAXB is a part of Java Web Services Developer Pack and provides a conceptually similar approach to XML façades, but differs in several details. To use JAXB serialization with Oracle BPEL Process Manager, take the following steps:

1. Add the JAXB JAR files, located in the JWSDP installation directory (for example `C:\jwsdp-1.5\jaxb\lib`) to the environment variable `BASE_OB_CLASSPATH` in the `obsetenv.bat` file found in `C:\OraBPELPM_1\integration\orabpel\bin` and to the `application.xml` file found in `C:\OraBPELPM_1\integration\orabpel\system\appserver\oc4j\j2ee\home\config`.

2. Copy the `JAXBSerializer.class` file (from the code download) into the `C:\OraBPELPM_1\integration\orabpel\system\classes\com\oracle\bpel\xml\util` directory.

3. Copy the Java classes produced by the JAXB compiler (`xjc`) to the `C:\OraBPELPM_1\integration\orabpel\system\classes` directory.

You also have to define which serializer your BPEL project will use. Do this in the `bpel.xml` file, where you have to define the `javaSerializer` property:

```
<partnerLinkBinding name="helper">
    <property name="wsdlLocation">HelperService.wsdl</property>
    <property name="javaSerializer">
      com.oracle.bpel.xml.util.JAXBSerializer</property>
</partnerLinkBinding>
```

XML beans are another approach for Java-to-XML bindings, originally developed by BEA, which donated the project to the Apache community. In contrast to XML façades and JAXB, XML beans provide an approach that does not completely hide XML from Java developers. Instead, it provides Java interfaces with getter/setter methods and additional methods through which you can manipulate XML directly if needed. XML beans are also aware of XML Infoset—when XML is converted to Java objects, the whole XML Infoset is available to the developer.

Similar to JAXB, you have to take a few configuration steps in order to use XML beans:

1. Add the XML beans JAR files (`xbean.jar` from BEA Weblogic) to the environment variable `BASE_OB_CLASSPATH` in the `obsetenv.bat` file found in `C:\OraBPELPM_1\integration\orabpel\bin` and to the `application.xml` file found in `C:\OraBPELPM_1\integration\orabpel\system\appserver\oc4j\j2ee\home\config`.

2. Copy the `XMLBeansSerializer.class` file (see the code download) into the `C:\OraBPELPM_1\integration\orabpel\system\classes\com\oracle\bpel\xml\util` directory.

3. Copy the Java classes produced by the XML beans compiler to the `C:\OraBPELPM_1\integration\orabpel\system\classes` directory.

4. Set path to the `xbean.jar` in the `build.xml` file used with the ANT utility (obant).

You also have to define which BPEL project should use the XML bean serializer, in the bpel.xml file:

```
<partnerLinkBinding name="xmlBeansService">
  <property name="wsdlLocation">XMLBeansService.wsdl</property>
  <property name="javaSerializer">
    com.oracle.bpel.xml.util.XMLBeanJavaSerializer
  </property>
</partnerLinkBinding>
```

The third well-known approach for Java to XML bindings is **Axis beans**, and you can use them with Oracle BPEL Process Manager too.

Similar to the previous two examples, you have to take a few configuration steps in order to use Axis beans:

1. Add the Axis beans JAR files (axis.jar from Axis version 1.2) to the environment variable BASE_OB_CLASSPATH in the obsetenv.bat file found in c:\OraBPELPM_1\ integration\orabpel\bin and to the application.xml file found in C:\OraBPELPM_1\integration\orabpel\system\appserver\oc4j\j2ee\home\ config.

2. Copy the serializer classes from AxisSerializer.zip (see the code download) into the C:\OraBPELPM_1\integration\orabpel\system\classes directory.

3. Copy the Java classes produced by Axis beans to the c:\OraBPELPM_1\ integration\orabpel\system\classes directory.

You also have to define which BPEL project should use the Axis bean serializer, in the bpel.xml file:

```
<partnerLinkBinding name="AxisBeansService">
  <property name="wsdlLocation">AxisBeansService.wsdl</property>
  <property name="javaSerializer">
      com.oracle.bpel.xml.util.AxisJavaSerializer
  </property>
</partnerLinkBinding>
```

WSIF Binding for EJBs

Now you know how to use a Java class instead of a web service through WSIF bindings. In a similar manner, you can use EJBs, particularly the stateless session beans. To demonstrate the WSIF EJB binding, we will extend our example. We will include an additional activity in our BPEL process; after invoking the Book Rating service, we will invoke the Publisher Rating service. Through WSIF binding we will use a session bean instead of a web service. We assume that the session bean already exists. To achieve this goal, we will go through several steps:

1. Define the WSDL for the session bean.
2. Add the partner link type to the WSDL.
3. Supplement the BPEL process to invoke the Publisher Rating service.
4. Add the WSIF binding to EJB.

WSDL for Session Bean

The session bean that we will use has the following remote component interface:

```
package com.oracle.ratingSB;

import java.rmi.RemoteException;
import javax.ejb.EJBObject;

public interface PubRating extends EJBObject
{
    public int getAvgPubRating (String name) throws RemoteException;

}
```

You can see that it provides a method called getAvgPubRating(), which takes a string as input and returns an integer. We will not show the home interface, the implementation class, and the deployment descriptors here (see the sample code).

Next define the corresponding WSDL document, which is very simple and defines two messages (PubRatingRequestMessage and PubRatingResponseMessage). They are used in the operation of PubRating as input and output. The operation is declared within the PubRatingPT port type:

```
<?xml version="1.0"?>
<definitions xmlns:xs="http://www.w3.org/2001/XMLSchema"
             xmlns:tns="http://oracle.com/service/pubrating/"
             targetNamespace="http://oracle.com/service/pubrating/"
             xmlns="http://schemas.xmlsoap.org/wsdl/"
             xmlns:plnk="http://schemas.xmlsoap.org/ws/2003/05/partner-link/"
             xmlns:format="http://schemas.xmlsoap.org/wsdl/formatbinding/"
             xmlns:ejb="http://schemas.xmlsoap.org/wsdl/ejb/" >

    <message name="PubRatingRequestMessage">
      <part name="name" type="xs:string" />
    </message>

    <message name="PubRatingResponseMessage">
      <part name="rating" type="xs:int" />
    </message>

    <portType name="PubRatingPT">
      <operation name="PubRating">
        <input name="PubRatingRequest" message="tns:PubRatingRequestMessage" />
        <output name="PubRatingResponse"
                message="tns:PubRatingResponseMessage" />
      </operation>
    </portType>
</definitions>
```

Add Partner Link Type

To use the WSDL, you have to add the partner link type. The operation is synchronous; therefore you need only one role:

```
<plnk:partnerLinkType name="PubRatingLT">
  <plnk:role name="PubRatingService">
    <plnk:portType name="tns:PubRatingPT" />
  </plnk:role>
</plnk:partnerLinkType>
```

Supplement BPEL Process

Now you are ready to supplement the BPEL process to invoke the Publisher Rating service. First, define a new partner link:

```
<partnerLink name="PubRating"
             partnerLinkType="pbr:PubRatingLT"
             partnerRole="PubRatingService"/>
```

Next, add the interaction with the Publisher Rating service as a new scope just after the Book Rating scope. Please notice that here you only add new functionality to BPEL:

```
<scope name="RetrievePublisherRating">

    <variables>
        <variable name="PubRatingRequest"
messageType="pbr:PubRatingRequestMessage"/>
        <variable name="PubRatingResponse"
messageType="pbr:PubRatingResponseMessage"/>
    </variables>

    <faultHandlers>

        <catchAll>

            <sequence>
              <assign>
                <copy>
                  <from expression="string('Unable to retrieve publisher rating')" />
                  <to variable="Fault" part="error" />
                </copy>
              </assign>

              <invoke partnerLink="Client"
                      portType="buy:ClientCallbackPT"
                      operation="ClientCallbackFault"
                      inputVariable="Fault" />
            </sequence>

        </catchAll>

    </faultHandlers>

    <sequence>

      <assign>
        <copy>
          <from variable="BookPurchase" part="book"
                query="/book/bkr:Publisher"/>
          <to variable="PubRatingRequest" part="name"/>
        </copy>
      </assign>

      <invoke partnerLink="PubRating"
              portType="pbr:PubRatingPT"
              operation="PubRating"
              inputVariable="PubRatingRequest"
              outputVariable="PubRatingResponse" />

    </sequence>

</scope>
```

Add WSIF Binding for EJB

WSIF EJB binding is similar to Java class binding, the major difference being that you have to specify the details regarding the mapping of WSDL operations to EJB methods.

What follows is the WSIF EJB binding excerpt from the Publisher Rating service WSDL file. We have first defined the type mapping and then specified which method should be used for the PubRating operation (getAvgPubRating()). Please notice that we have specified the message part names for parameters (name) and for return (rating). We have also specified the input and output message names (PubRatingRequest and PubRatingResponse respectively):

```
<binding name="EJBBinding" type="tns:PubRatingPT">
  <ejb:binding/>
  <format:typeMapping encoding="Java" style="Java">
    <format:typeMap typeName="xs:string" formatType="java.lang.String" />
    <format:typeMap typeName="xs:int" formatType="int" />
  </format:typeMapping>
  <operation name="PubRating">
    <ejb:operation
        methodName="getAvgPubRating"
        parameterOrder="name"
        interface="remote"
        returnPart="rating" />
    <input name="PubRatingRequest"/>
    <output name="PubRatingResponse"/>
  </operation>
</binding>
```

In the services binding you have to specify additional details of the EJB such as JNDI name, JNDI provider URL, and initial context factory. The JNDI provider URL is specific for each deployment. In this case it would be ormi://localhost/SessionBean. You can use the obant utility to replace the [jndiProviderURL] with the actual address at the time of deployment (please look in the build.xml file for details):

```
<service name="PubRatingPT">
  <port name="EJBPort" binding="tns:EJBBinding">
    <ejb:address className="com.oracle.ratingSB.PubRatingHome"
                jndiName="ejb/session/PubRating"
                initialContextFactory=
                        "com.evermind.server.rmi.RMIInitialContextFactory"
                jndiProviderURL="[jndiProviderURL]"/>
  </port>
</service>
```

Now you are almost ready to deploy the example and test it. Don't forget to add the wsdlLocation property to the bpel.xml deployment descriptor:

```
<partnerLinkBinding name="PubRating">
  <property name="wsdlLocation">PubRatingBinded.wsdl</property>
</partnerLinkBinding>
```

Please note that you could use the deployment descriptor to add additional properties required by the EJB, such as java.naming.security.principal and java.naming.security.credentials, if your EJB would require authentication and authorization:

```
<partnerLinkBinding name="PubRating">
  <property name="wsdlLocation">PubRatingBinded.wsdl</property>
  <property name="java.naming.security.principal">admin</property>
  <property name="java.naming.security.credentials">welcome</property>
</partnerLinkBinding>
```

To test the example, you first have to deploy the session bean and then the BPEL process. Again, use obant, which automates the procedure:

```
Z:\WSIF\4_JavaBindingEJB>obant

Z:\WSIF\4_JavaBindingEJB>SETLOCAL
Buildfile: build.xml

deploySessionBean:

build_ear:

deployIas:

deployOc4j:
     [java] Notification ==> Application Deployer for SessionBean STARTS [
2005-
10-19T19:47:00.891CEST ]
     [java] Notification ==> Undeploy previous deployment
     [java] Notification ==> Copy the archive to
C:\OraBPELPM_1\integration\orabpel\system\appserver\oc4j\j2ee\home\application
s\SessionBean.ear
     [java] Notification ==> Unpack SessionBean.ear begins...
     [java] Notification ==> Unpack SessionBean.ear ends...
     [java] Notification ==> Initialize SessionBean.ear begins...
     [java] Notification ==> Initialize SessionBean.ear ends...
     [java] Notification ==> Application Deployer for SessionBean COMPLETES [
2005-10-19T19:47:19.470CEST ]


bindingWsdl:
     [copy] Copying 1 file to Z:\WSIF\4_JavaBindingEJB

setJndiUrlOrclej2ee:

setJndiUrlIas:

setJndiUrlOc4j:
     [echo] Replacing token [jndiProviderURL] by ormi://virtualxp/SessionBean
in
 Z:\WSIF\4_JavaBindingEJB/PubRatingBinded.wsdl

main:
     [bpelc] validating "Z:\WSIF\4_JavaBindingEJB\BuyBook.bpel" ...
     [bpelc] BPEL suitcase deployed to:
C:\OraBPELPM_1\integration\orabpel\domains\default\deploy

all:

BUILD SUCCESSFUL
Total time: 28 seconds

Z:\WSIF\4_JavaBindingEJB>ENDLOCAL

Z:\WSIF\4_JavaBindingEJB>
```

After starting the BPEL process from the console, you should see that the Publisher Rating service has been invoked:

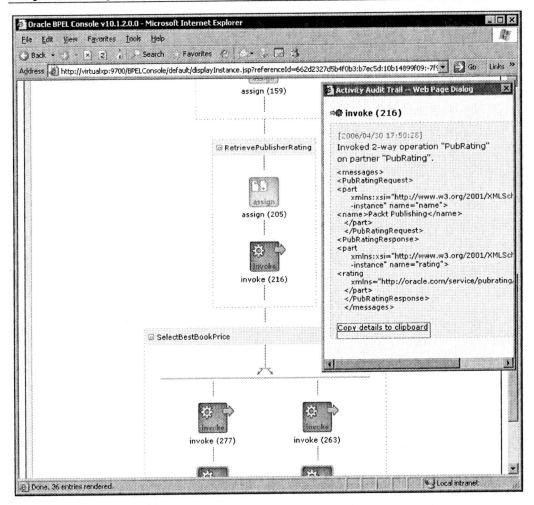

To be absolutely sure that the EJB has been invoked, have a look at the BPEL server console windows; you should see the following output:

```
05/10/19 19:50:51 Tutalii: C:\OraBPELPM_1\integration\orabpel\lib\orabpel.jar ar
chive
05/10/19 19:50:54 Avg. publisher rating for Packt Publishing: 5.
```

Generating WSIF Bindings from JDeveloper

Writing WSIF bindings by hand can be quite complicated; therefore, Oracle JDeveloper 10.1.3 provides a wizard for automatic generation of WSDL and WSIF for existing Java resources, such as Java classes and EJBs. This greatly reduces the effort to invoke Java resources from BPEL and makes BPEL even more attractive for integration.

Based on a Java class or EJB, you have to start the wizard for the creation of a Java web service. The screenshots apply to a Java class example:

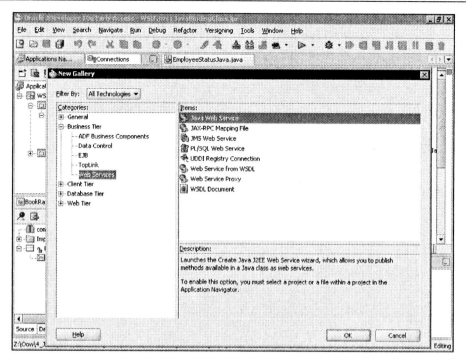

Select the JAX-RPC web service type that is J2EE 1.4 compliant.

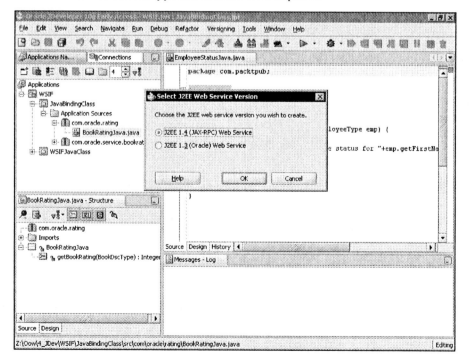

Next, select the Java class or the stateless session bean you would like to use. Check the WSIF binding option (to generate WSIF binding).

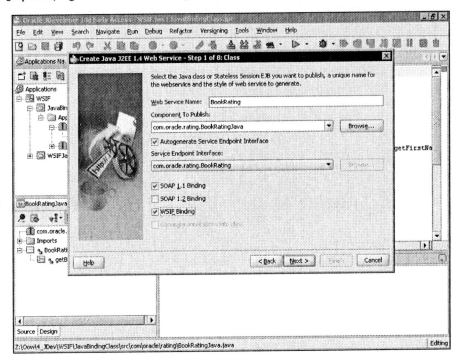

Next select the SOAP message format, where you can use Document/Wrapped, Document/Literal, RPC/Literal, or RPC/Encoded representations.

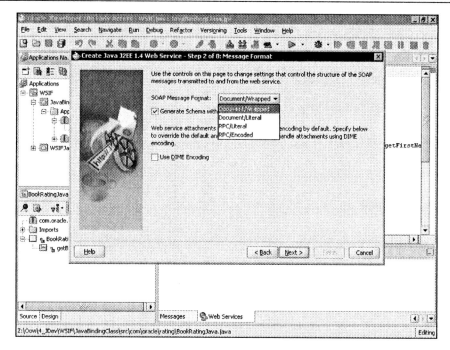

Next, specify custom mappings between XML types and their Java equivalent classes, and the corresponding serializers for the mapping.

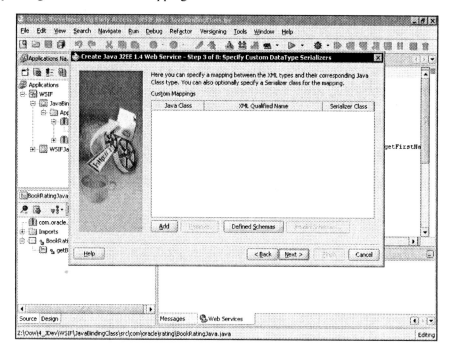

Specify the namespaces used by the web services.

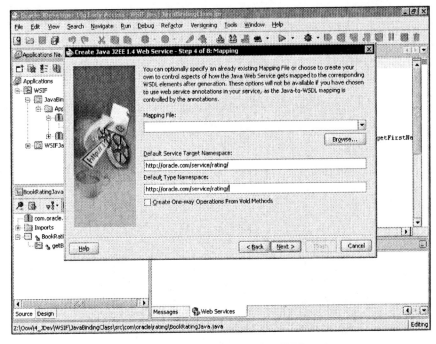

Finally, select the methods that should be exposed through WSDL:

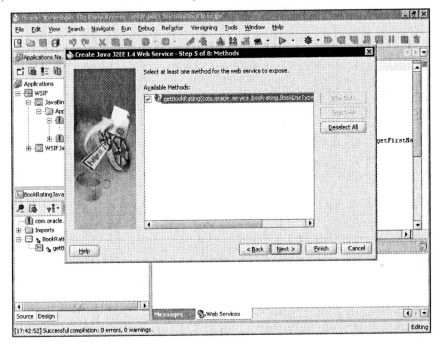

The wizard offers additional steps where you specify the optional class loaders, JAX-RPC handler classes, service state (stateful), and additional classes used by the service. In most cases you will not need to specify these; so you can conclude the wizard by pressing the Finish button and look at the generated WSDL, where you will find the WSIF bindings, similar to those written by hand. Refer to the JDeveloper documentation for more information on the wizard.

Conclusion

As you've learned through various examples here, WSIF offers EAI-like capabilities as well as the flexibility to configure partner services of BPEL processes in an easy and flexible way. Clearly, WSIF extends the usability of BPEL to existing resources and makes BPEL an even more valuable technology for SOA.

BPEL with Reliable Processing

by Jeremy Bolie and Michael Cardella

Learn how to build a reusable, highly reliable business process using BPEL.

As web services and BPEL processes proliferate within an organization, quality of service becomes a distinguishing factor in the adoption of a particular service. How do you ensure that the requested functionality will be completed by the service despite all obstacles, such as network failure or unavailable applications? Can the service be leveraged across different business processes? Answers to all these questions determine the reusability of a particular business process. The more robust the business process is, the higher the reusability of the process across multiple applications.

In this chapter of *The BPEL Cookbook*, we will describe a business scenario comprising multiple applications. This scenario demonstrates the need for a BPEL process capable of providing functionality with assurance and how this BPEL process will be leveraged multiple times in different business scenarios. It then walks you through a step-by-step process of building a BPEL process that offers this high quality of service through intelligent retry logic. You also learn how this process can be enhanced through superior exception management, email-based notification, and error logging.

Business Scenario

Reusability of a service is the cornerstone of any service-oriented architecture (SOA) strategy. Organizations can derive the true value of any SOA implementation only if they can create a set of reusable services. These services will then be used by different departments or applications in different business contexts. In addition to the actual business value provided, reusability of a specific service is driven by the success history of the service. What is its failure rate? Does it have the ability to overcome network interruptions? Is the service resilient enough to recover from errors and exceptions? The higher the assurance the service can provide about its ability to complete the requested job, the better its chances are of being leveraged in different business contexts.

Consider the scenario shown in the figure that follows: An enterprise needs to provision technical documentation of its products to its various partners. The level of access to the documentation depends on the partner type and the product documentation being requested. This information is stored in an Oracle database. As partners join and leave the network, provisioning information is modified (access is added/updated/deleted) through appropriate approvals and updates in multiple enterprise applications.

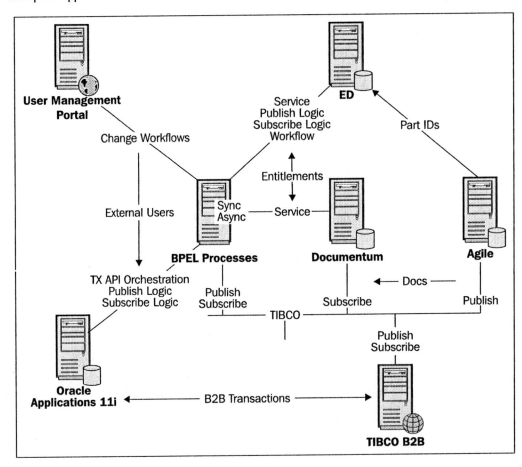

As entitlements are activated, deactivated, and modified in the entitlements database, notifications must be sent to the documentation service, Documentum. The order in which the entitlement changes are sent must match the order in which they are created. It is critical that no messages are lost, and a complete audit log must be maintained and logged to a central application database log.

BPEL can play a vital role in orchestrating the entitlement activation and deactivation. This BPEL process will work closely with the TIBCO messaging bus to deliver the messages reliably to Documentum. It will also be responsible for error logging and notification. The process has to perform the task efficiently and reliably enough that network interruptions or the unavailability of a Documentum application doesn't break it down. It should be capable of trying again and again to perform its task to completion. How do you develop such a BPEL process with reliable processing?

The rest of this chapter details a strategy for improving the quality of service of processing, using BPEL. A key aspect of creating retries with data processing is the database. This strategy should be just one piece of the puzzle in improving the reliability and quality of service of the processes running in BPEL.

Architecture

Let's take a look at the logic for designing such a BPEL process.

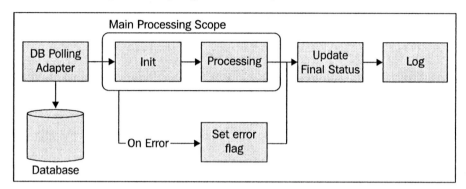

This BPEL process, which reads a record from the database and process it, is kicked off by Oracle BPEL's database polling adapter. One of the last steps of the BPEL process is to report a success or a failure back to the database. This database procedure then determines if the process needs to be retried, based on both the status and number of retry attempts made, and if it does need to be retried, it reschedules the record to be picked up in the future. The final step in the process is to call the log service. In addition to creating a log entry in the database, this service uses a set of rules that determines if a message with a certain status from a given process should have a notification sent out. If so, it also identifies the email template to use and the distribution list for the email, to which the appropriate information in the log gets added.

This improves the reliability both in cases where the problem may be self-correcting and in cases where human interaction may be needed to fix the problem. In contrast to the partner retry, this approach retries the entire execution of the BPEL process. It is more feature-rich than just creating a simple retry loop within BPEL.

This processing model is easy to externally monitor and interact with. If you manage the create date and last-modified date of the process in the database, it is possible to run queries against the database to see:

- Which records are not getting picked up by BPEL
- Which ones have not completed their processing in a timely manner
- Which ones have been aborted

Additionally, it is easy to initiate a retry of an aborted record and expedite a scheduled retry.

Here are three important things you should do in implementing the above design:

1. Have the status of the record being processed stored in the database. The status includes the process state, next process attempt time, and processing attempt count.

2. Create an updatable view that exposes only records that are ready to be processed. A view is needed because the database adapter cannot handle a where clause that compares against SYSDATE.

3. Design logic that determines if a process instance that has faulted should be retried, and when the retry should occur. This information will be updated in the database by use of a stored procedure. This can also be done with an update partner link and additional logic in BPEL.

In the next section, you learn how to build such a process.

Building the Sample

Let's build the process we just described. First, you create the database tables to support the process, and then you use the BPEL PM Designer to model the process.

Creating the Database Objects

Because the process stores the retry status in the database, you need to design the database component before creating the BPEL process. As discussed earlier, the main database additions that need to be made are:

*   More fields to track the status of records being processed
*   Updatable view
*   Status procedure

The additional fields can be added to the row that contains the data being modified or to a parallel table with a one-to-one relationship to the main table. The main columns that should be added are:

*   Status
*   Process Not Before
*   Retry Count
*   Create DTS
*   Last Modified DTS

The status field should be the same one that is used by BPEL's database polling adapter to identify unprocessed records. It is helpful to create a convention to make it easy to identify records that are still being processed, those that completed successfully, and those that completed with an error. A couple of ways to do this are by using number ranges or a prefix convention. Check CREATE_TB_DB_POLL_SOURCE.sql in the sample code download.

The view should then expose only records whose Process Not Before column entry is earlier than the current SYSDATE or is null. This is also an easy place to limit the number of records that should be processed. The view can also expose only the primary key of the record to be processed, making the view more lightweight. Check CREATE_VW_DB_POLL_SOURCE_VW.sql in the attached sample.

The status procedure should have a flag to indicate an error, or a separate procedure can be used to identify an error state. For the error state, the procedure should identify whether the process instance should be retried, and if so, when. It then should update the record accordingly. The typical strategy is to retry a few times with a short interval between tries and then go to a larger number of retries with a much longer interval. Check SET_DB_POLL_SOURCE_FAULTED.sql in the sample code download.

Next, you create the actual BPEL process to handle the database record in a reliable manner.

Creating the DB Polling Process

This involves several steps:

1. **Create a new BPEL project**:
   Create an empty BPEL project.

2. **Create a DB polling adapter**:

   a. Create a new partner link.

   b. Click the Wizard button.

   c. Select Database Wizard.

   d. Assign the service name DBPolling.

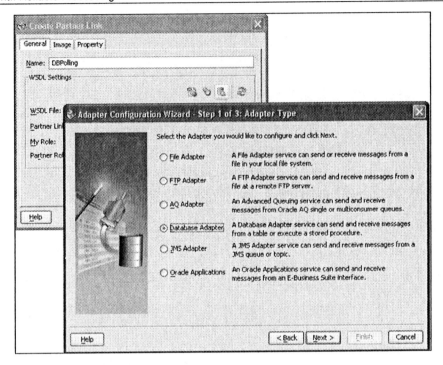

e. After configuring database connection, select Poll for New or Changed Records in a Table as the operation type.

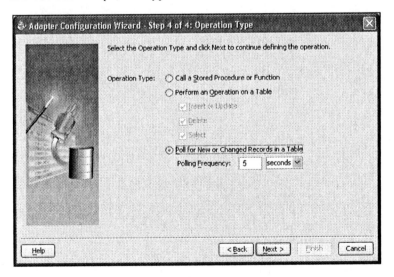

f. Import the DB view DB_POLL_SOURCE_VW.

g. Accept the defaults in succeeding screens (no "where" clause in this example). Pick the column ID as the primary key.

h. After the read is performed on the view, the wizard needs to know what should be done with the records. Select Update a Field in the DbPollSource Table (Logical Delete), as shown in the following screenshot:

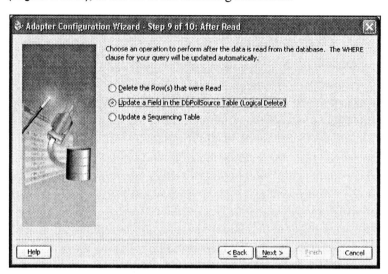

i. Now you are on the Logical Delete screen. Specify the BPEL_STATE field to be updated to logically delete the row.

3. **Create a receive activity**
   To add a receive activity to the BPEL process:

   a. Drag the receive connector to the DBPolling partner link created in step 2.

   b. Rename the receive activity receive.

   c. Check the Create Instance checkbox.

   d. Click the variable wizard on the receive activity pop-up menu, and create a variable named inputVariable.

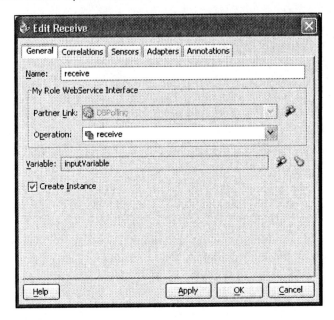

   e. Click OK.

   The BPEL process will look something like the following figure:

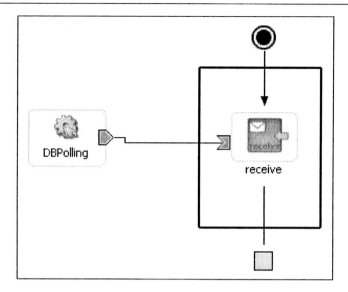

The BPEL Processes Images in this chapter have been edited for clarity purposes. Actual BPEL process will look slightly different in BPEL Designer.

4. **Add the custom fault definition**:
   A prerequisite for adding the custom fault is that the WSDL that contains the fault definition must be referenced by one of the partner link's WSDLs. Although it is possible to modify any of the partner link's WSDLs, the partner link's WSDLs will be regenerated if the wizard is rerun. This means that the step of adding the import to the WSDL will need to be repeated if the wizard is rerun.

   To add BpelFault.wsdl to the project folder:

   a. Select the project in Oracle JDeveloper, select File | Add to DB_to_JMS.jpr, and select BpelFault.wsdl to be added.

   b. Add the following line to DBPollingService.wsdl, after the opening definitions tag and before the types element:

   ```
   <import
   namespace="http://schemas.oracle.com/otn/bpel/sample/dbpoll/jmspub/fault"
           location="BpelFault.wsdl"/>
   ```

   This WSDL uses message parts, rather than a single complex element, for each part of the data, to allow this same fault definition to be usable as the fault return type from BPEL. Without the message part section of the WSDL, BPEL creates an RPC-style web service rather than a document-style one.

5. **Create the rest of the BPEL process**:
   Instead of walking through the remaining steps of building the BPEL process, let's see what the final process looks like and then get the individual elements. The entire BPEL process is shown in the following figure:

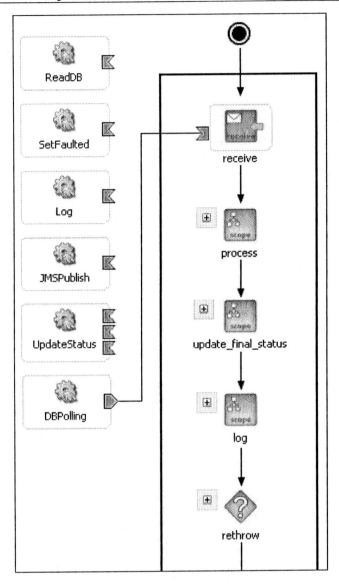

Let's consider the individual elements of this BPEL process. The key pieces are

- Init block (within process scope)
- Processing
- Reply/report final status
- Logging
- Rethrow fault

Init Block

This is the first set of tasks inside the processing scope. As the name suggests, it is responsible for process initialization and setting global, error, and log variables. As shown in the following figure, the following activities are included in the sample code download.

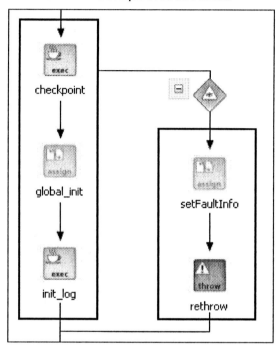

- **checkpoint (optional)**
  The checkpoint forces dehydration. Although it slows execution slightly, it guarantees that every BPEL process instance started will show up in the console.

  The BPEL Console shows the state of execution only up to the last dehydration point. Some errors kill execution without allowing the state to be reported to the console. Also, some partner link synchronous calls can wait indefinitely, never allowing a dehydration state to be reported.

- **global_init**
  This assign initializes a few "constants" that are used by the exception handling mechanism. This needs to happen toward the beginning of the process, before anything that has any potential to throw a fault.

- **init_log**
  The init_log task initializes a time in Java so that the approximate processing time can easily be tracked, down to the millisecond. This is needed only if the process is integrated with a logging system that will be collecting execution time down to the millisecond.

Processing

Now we're at the heart of the processing. Take a look at the following BPEL process flow.

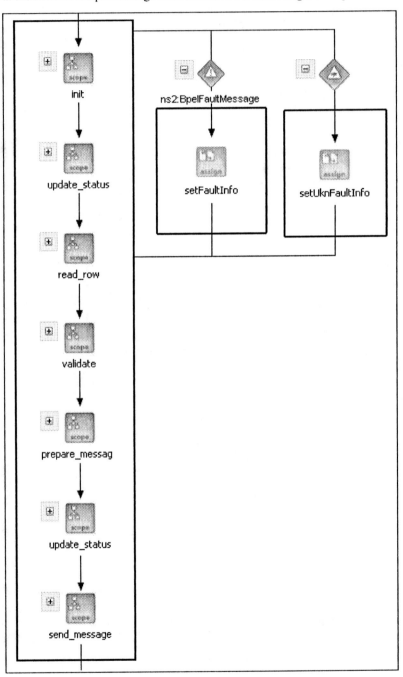

Process Flow

After initializing the variables, the process begins reading the database. It updates the current status to "processing" and then reads the database record. After verifying the correctness of the data, it transforms the message for destination delivery. Before sending the message to the destination, it updates the current status in the database to "sending". Finally, it sends the message to the destination (the JMS bus, in this case). That the process updates the status in the database as it traverses the key points in the flow is especially useful if the process is long-running or has some key risk areas. The read from the database (ReadDB partner link) has been separated from the view that initiates the process (DBPolling partner link). This keeps the view simple and gets past the limitation that joins cannot be used against the views in BPEL.

Exception Handling

Each scope contained in a larger scope catches all the exceptions and throws an internally defined fault. For example, when there is an error during the reading of the database record, the scope will catch this error, set the error status as "Error while trying to read in data to be processed", and throw this error to the parent scope. This means that every fault is localized to a finer level.

Whenever an error occurs inside the main processing, a fault of internal type is thrown. An outer catch block then catches this fault. One thing to be careful about when using this strategy is not to catch a custom fault in a catchall block, which causes all the custom fault information to be lost. If a custom fault is thrown within a scope, a catch block catching that specific fault should be used in addition to a catchall block that will catch any other errors.

Reusability

It's important to note that the processing logic is based on business needs. In this scenario, this process is providing message delivery to the JMS destination in a reliable manner. However, in real life, processing can vary from updating a bank account to creating a new customer, to synchronizing order data. The reliability offered by this process remains the same. The process can also be reused in a reliable manner.

Reply/Report Final Status

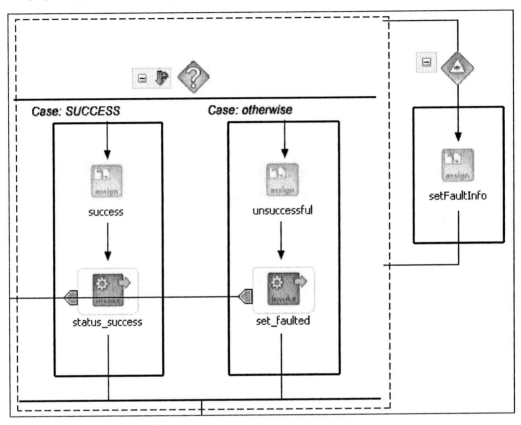

The processing status is updated in the database, to either success or the fault encountered during the process, as shown in the screenshot. Although this update is optional, it is recommended to enable an outside application to monitor the progress of all the process instances from start to end.

In this example, the reporting of the final status is done with a database procedure (SetFaulted partner link). Although the reporting can be done inside BPEL, deferring the update to a database procedure simplifies the BPEL process.

A report that the final status is unsuccessful triggers a retry of the process. If the process has not been retried the maximum number of times, it will be retried after a certain interval.

Logging

The logging process gathers processing information and sends it to the centralized logger. The most important part of that information is the severity of the error and the message code. Logging provides the following benefits:

- It generates an audit log that is easily searchable through the database.
- The severity and the message code determine whether to send out a notification.
- The message contains some key pieces of information such as the BPEL process instance and the primary key for the row that kicked off the processing. This allows a troubleshooter quickly to locate the process in the BPEL Console, or the data in the database.

Rethrow Fault

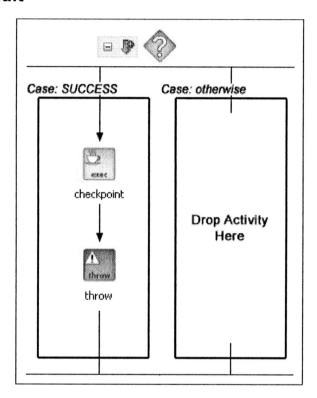

As shown in the figure, the final rethrow simplifies the identification of problematic process instances. These process instances are relatively easy to locate in the BPEL Console. When a fault is rethrown at the end, the process instances get flagged in the console, and you can also filter to show just the processes that ended with a fault (Canceled).

This completes the development of the BPEL process. This process should be combined with other practices to provide the best reliability; examples include database monitoring, synthetic transactions, and log monitoring. The process enables you to easily identify the records that have succeeded, ended with a fault, or not completed their processing in a timely manner. All this information is very helpful in a real-life business environment in which each record being processed can be worth thousands of dollars, and SLA violations can result in unhappy customers.

Conclusion

This chapter has demonstrated how to build a reusable business process that performs its task with high reliability. The process you built sends a message to the JMS destination in a reliable manner, and given its high degree of reusability, it can be used to provide any business functionality in a reliable manner.

Not all business exceptions can be caught in a BPEL process. Offering high quality of service does not end at the process level. It has to be combined with efficient monitoring of audit logs, notifying appropriate stakeholders, troubleshooting exceptions at the data and process level, and enabling transparency at every stage of processing. Any reliable process should address all these requirements.

10

Managing a BPEL Production Environment

by Stany Blanvalet

Learn how to automate common admin tasks in a BPEL production environment using BPEL Process Manager's API and Dehydration Store.

Some organizations spend as much as 70% of their IT budget to maintain and administer current IT functionality and operations. But paradoxically, managing the performance and availability of web services is not a high priority for most companies implementing service-oriented architecture (SOA). Thus, as organizations adopt web services and BPEL to build SOA infrastructure, it is becoming more and more imperative to design new strategies to decrease the costs of application management and administration.

This goal is particularly important for BPEL implementations, in which multiple business processes are often deployed to the production environment. As more and more processes are deployed in the production environment, efficient administration becomes increasingly important. Every BPEL process that has completed its execution, successfully or not, is stored in the database, as is every XML message that is exchanged between different steps in the process flow. As you might expect, this process causes the database to grow in size exponentially, thereby leading to performance bottlenecks.

For these reasons, in your BPEL production environment, it's important that you have the ability to:

- Archive information about completed BPEL processes without affecting the stability of the production system
- Remove all XML messages that have been successfully delivered and resolved from the database
- Delete stale instances
- Rerun failed processes

In this installment of *The BPEL Cookbook*, you will learn how BPEL Process Manager's APIs and Dehydration Store enable these capabilities, as well as strategies for archiving and deleting information about completed instances of a BPEL process. You will also learn how to delete stale instances and complete invoke and callback XML messages using PL/SQL and EJB. Finally, you will learn how to rerun failed process instances via the BPELTest utility.

BPEL Process Manager API and Dehydration Store

Oracle BPEL Process Manager Console provides a user-friendly, web-based interface for management, administration, and debugging of processes deployed to the BPEL server. However, in production environments, administrators need strong control over management tasks. Via a PL/SQL query or BPEL API against the BPEL Dehydration Store database, it is possible to automate most of these administrative tasks. But before creating action items, it's important to understand the concepts underlying the Dehydration Store and BPEL Process Manager API.

The Dehydration Store database is used to store process status data, especially for asynchronous BPEL processes. Here's a quick overview of some its more important tables:

Table	Contents
CUBE_INSTANCE	Instance metadata information (creation date, current state, process ID)
CUBE_SCOPE	Scope data for an instance
AUDIT_TRAIL	Audit trail information for an instance; this information can be viewed from BPEL Console
AUDIT_DETAILS	Large detailed audit information about a process instance
DLV_MESSAGE	Callback message metadata
DLV_MESSAGE_BIN	Payload of callback messages
INVOKE_MESSAGE	Invocation messages metadata
INVOKE_MESSAGE_BIN	Payload of invocation messages
DLV_SUBSCRIPTION	Delivery subscriptions for an instance
TASK	Tasks created for an instance (i.e. title, assignee, status, expiration)

The database schema can be found in the DDL script domain_oracle.dll in the $ORABPEL$\integration\orabpel\system\database\scripts directory. With proper knowledge of this schema, administrators can bypass the BPEL Console and write SQL queries against the store directly.

In addition to the SQL approach, administrators can leverage the BPEL Process Manager API. This API provides an exhaustive set of classes to find, archive, or delete instances in various states, delete callback/invoke messages across different domains, or query on the status of a specific domain, process, or instance. (API documentation is available at $ORABPEL$\integration\orabpel\docs\apidocs\index.html.) The following table summarizes some of the most relevant classes/interfaces and corresponding methods here.

Class/Interface	Methods
Class whereConditionHelper	Provides methods such as whereInstancesClosed(), whereInstancesStale(), and whereInstancesOpen(), which construct a where clause that searches for respective instances.
Interface IBPELDomainHandle	Allows the developer to perform operations on a running BPEL process domain. Provides methods such as archiveAllInstances(), deleteAllInstances(), deleteInstancesByProcessId(), deployProcess(), undeployPorcess(), deleteAllHandledCallback(), and deleteAllHandledInvoke().
Interface IinstanceHandle	Allows the user to perform operations on an active instance. Provides methods such as isStale(), getState(), getModifyDate(), and delete().
Class Locator	Allows the user to search for processes, instances, and activities that have been deployed and instantiated within an Orabpel process domain. Provides methods such as listInstances() and listActivities(), and can take where clauses as parameters.

Next, you'll learn how to perform some of the most important administrative tasks.

Archiving Completed Instances

As explained previously, all successfully executed process instances are stored in the Dehydration Store. Currently a BPEL instance is saved in two tables after the instance is completed: cube_instance and cube_scope. The former stores the instance header information: domain, creation date, state (completed, running, stale, and canceled), priority, title, and so on. The latter stores the state of the instance (variable values and so on). By default, both tables are used to store a completed instance.

Purging the instance information from the database can be accomplished from the BPEL Console as shown in the following screenshot:

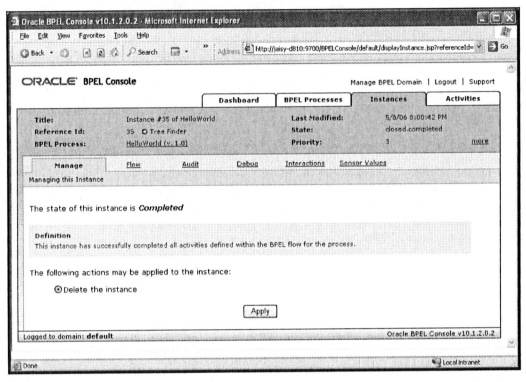

In a production environment, it will be necessary to archive the information before you delete the information—and to do so for hundreds of instances. Fortunately, you can achieve this goal using PL/SQL or EJB. (Remember to move the information to a different location before purging it from the BPEL database.) Let's look at some examples.

Archiving with EJB

For this example we will use the following interface and method.

com.oracle.bpel.client	Interface IBPELDomainHandle
Method Summary	
int	archiveInstances(WhereCondition wc, boolean deleteInstances)
	(Archives all instances returned by the search condition specified by wc.)

The method archiveInstances will archive and delete all completed instances. It accepts the parameter keepdays, which indicates how old a completed instance can be before it is archived.

```
public static int archiveInstances(Locator locator, String processId, int
keepdays)
   throws ORABPELAccessException {
      try {
         WhereCondition wc = WhereConditionHelper.whereInstancesClosed();
         WhereCondition tmpWhere = new WhereCondition();
         NonSyncStringBuffer buf = new NonSyncStringBuffer();
         if (!"*".equals(processId)) {
            buf.setLength(0);
            tmpWhere.setClause(buf.append(" AND ").append(
               SQLDefs.AL_ci_process_id).append(" = ? ").toString());
            tmpWhere.setString(1, processId);
            wc.append(tmpWhere);
         }
         Calendar cal = Calendar.getInstance();
         cal.add(Calendar.DATE, -keepdays);
         buf.setLength(0);
         tmpWhere.setClause(buf.append(" AND ").append(
            SQLDefs.AL_ci_modify_date).append(" <= ? ").toString());
         tmpWhere.setTimestamp(1, cal.getTime());
         wc.append(tmpWhere);
         IBPELDomainHandle domain = locator.lookupDomain();
         return domain.archiveInstances(wc, true);
      } catch (ServerException se) {
         throw new ORABPELAccessException(se.getMessage());
      }
   }
}
```

Archiving with PL/SQL

Administrators can also leverage PL/SQL to accomplish this goal. Before deleting the records from the database, the DBA can move the record to a different database/table per their requirements. Here's an example:

```
Query: SELECT CIKEY FROM CUBE_INSTANCE, DOMAIN
       WHERE BPELMNG.CUBE_INSTANCE.DOMAIN_REF = BPELMNG.DOMAIN.DOMAIN_REF
       AND BPELMNG.DOMAIN.DOMAIN_ID = 'XXX'      ? XXX is the name of the domain
       AND STATE = 5                 ? '5' mean COMPLETED
       AND MODIFY_DATE < SYSDATE-X        ? X is the number of day of history
       AND PROCESS_ID = 'XXX';        ? XXX is the process name

Actions:
       For each CIKEY, call COLLAXA.delete_ci(CIKEY); oracle procedure.
```

In the next section, you'll learn how to delete callback and invoke messages.

Deleting Callback and Invoke Messages

Whenever an instance expects a message from a partner (receive, onMessage, and so on), a subscription is issued for that specific receive activity. Once a delivery message is received, the delivery layer attempts to correlate the message with the intended subscription. Successfully subscribed messages continue to remain in the database. These messages are deleted via the collaxa.delete_ci(CIKEY) stored procedure (as performed previously for instance archiving).

The same is true for all callback and invocation XML messages. All such messages remain in the database even if they have been successfully resolved and delivered.

You can use the following methods to delete all callbacks, invokes, and subscriptions.

com.oracle.bpel.client	Interface IBPELDomainHandle
Method Summary	
int	deleteAllHandledCallback () (Deletes all callback messages delivered to this domain that have been successfully resolved and delivered.)
int	DeleteAllHandledInvoke () (Deletes all invocation messages delivered to this domain that have been successfully resolved and delivered.)
int	DeleteAllHandledSubscription () (Deletes all message subscribers in this domain that have been successfully resolved and handled—that is, have had a message delivered to them.)

You can also use PL/SQL to do the same thing, as illustrated by the following stored procedures. I recommend that your DBA use this script as a starting point and modify it to suit specific archiving needs (deleting, moving to another database, altering the where clause to include a selection based on business criteria, and so on.)

```
/**
 * Procedure to clean invocation messages for a particular domain.
 * Invocation messages are stored in invoke_message and invoke_message_bin table
 * It will select all the invocation messages from invoke_message table.
 * For each message which has been delivered or resolved, delete it from
 * invoke_message and invoke_message_bin table
 */
    procedure delete_invoke( p_domain_ref in integer )
    as
      cursor c_invoke_message is
        select message_guid
        from invoke_message
        where ( state = 2 or state = 3 )
          and domain_ref = p_domain_ref
        for update;
    begin
        for r_invoke_message in c_invoke_message loop
        delete from invoke_message_bin
        where message_guid = r_invoke_message.message_guid;
        delete from invoke_message where current of c_invoke_message;
        end loop;
        commit;
    end delete_invoke;


/**
 * Procedure to clean callback messages for a particular domain.
 * Callback messages are stored in dlv_message and dlv_message_bin table
 * It will select all the invocation messages from dlv_message table.
 * For each message which has been delivered or resolved, delete it from
 * dlv_message and dlv_message_bin table
 */
```

```
procedure delete_callback( p_domain_ref in integer )
as
  cursor c_dlv_message is
    select message_guid
    from dlv_message
    where ( state = 2 or state = 3 )
      and domain_ref = p_domain_ref
    for update;
  begin
    for r_dlv_message in c_dlv_message loop
    delete from dlv_message_bin
    where message_guid = r_dlv_message.message_guid;
    delete from dlv_message
    where current of c_dlv_message;
    end loop;
    commit;
end delete_callback;
```

Next, let's take a look at how to delete stale instances.

Deleting Stale Instances

Using BPEL Console, you can identify all stale instances and kill them as shown in the following screenshot:

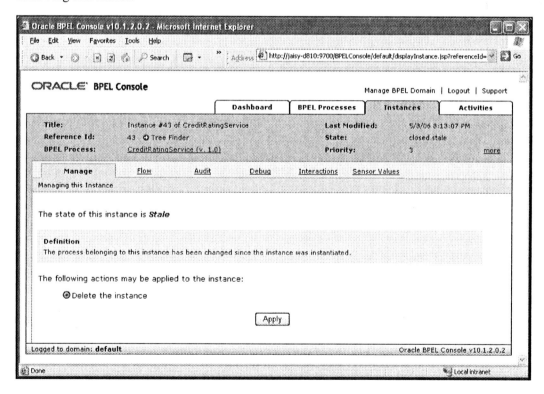

Unfortunately, these stale instances can be searched for only on a specific domain. However, in a production environment, multiple processes will probably be deployed across different domains—resulting in a huge administrative burden. Besides, purging all stale instances at once within a specific domain is not possible.

As an alternative approach, you can find a unique cube instance key (cikey) for every stale instance via the following SQL query:

```
SELECT CUBE_INSTANCE.cikey, CUBE_INSTANCE.root_id, CUBE_INSTANCE.process_id,

CUBE_INSTANCE.domain_ref
FROM CUBE_INSTANCE
WHERE STATE = 9
```

Once you have identified a CI key for each stale instance, you can use that key to delete stale instances from CUBE_INSTANCE and other tables that reference the cube instances by invoking delete_ci(CIKEY) for every cube instance found via the SQL query. delete_ci(CIKEY) is a stored procedure that takes a cube instance as a parameter, and deletes the cube instance and all rows on other BPEL tables that reference the cube instance.

One benefit of this approach is that stale instances can be deleted across multiple domains (if you remove the domain clause in the where condition). It also permits mass purging of stale instances. These two benefits make PL/SQL a strong candidate for managing the production environment.

The following sample code demonstrates how these methods can be used in an EJB to list and delete stale instances:

```
WhereCondition where = WhereConditionHelper.whereInstancesStale();
    IInstanceHandle[] instances = getLocator(domainId,
domainPassword).listInstances(where);
        for(int i=0; i<instances.length; i++){
            instances[i].delete();
    }
```

The first two lines return an array of the IInstanceHandle bean for all stale instances per domain. You then use IInstanceHandle.delete() to delete all these instances. You can easily extend this code to cover all domains.

Archiving old instances and deleting stale instances and handled XML messages will help reduce the size of the tables. It turns out that unless you either truncate or rebuild the table, just deleting rows does not put the free space back into the table space.

Use the following commands to regain that free space; similar commands can be executed for other tables in the Dehydration Store.

```
alter table cube_scope enable row movement;
alter table cube_scope shrink space compact;
alter table cube_scope shrink space;
alter table cube_scope disable row movement;
```

In addition, to prevent future growth, the DBA can manipulate the PCTFREE, PCTUSED, and PCTVERSION parameters.

Finally, let's see how to deal with instances that fail during run time.

Rerunning Failed Instances

BPEL processes may fail for multiple reasons—wrong input, incorrect process design, or an unavailable external application, just to name a few. In any case, the process will not successfully complete its execution and end up in a 'fault' state. If the process has failed due to incorrect design, you will have to modify the process design and redeploy the BPEL process.

However, if a process has failed due to incorrect input or external issues (network failure, unavailable external application), you would want to rerun the process once input has been corrected or external issues have been addressed. Ideally, you would rerun the process with the old inputs so that the original request is handled properly.

This goal can be accomplished using BPELTest (available in 10.1.3 and later), an important utility designed to create and run test cases on BPEL processes for unit and integration testing. BPELTest can simulate partner invocation, perform assertions, and provide information on various test results. (For more information, view the BPELTest webinar, listed at `http://www.oracle.com/technology/products/ias/bpel/htdocs/webinars.html`.)

The most relevant aspect of BPELTest is its ability to create a test case from an audit trail, also known as Automatic Test Generation. For example, consider a situation where a process instance fails in its execution because the external application is down. Ideally, you would like to rerun the process in exactly the same scenario when the external application is back online. This approach could be cumbersome, however; it would involve reconfiguring external dependencies that may or may not be controlled by the process owner.

Instead, using BPELTest, you can generate the basic test case from the audit trail of a failed instance. The generated test case will contain commands to emulate partners exactly as the failed instance had. In the case of incorrect data, you could modify the test case for correct data. If the failed instance were due to an unavailable external application, you could simply run the test case whenever the application is back up.

Conclusion

As you can see, it is possible to partially automate the management of a BPEL production environment using the BPEL Process Manager API and EJB or PL/SQL against the BPEL Dehydration Store. As you deploy more and more BPEL processes, it will become imperative to design a repository of utilities that automate everyday tasks and proactively address potential production issues.

Index

O

OA Adapter. *See* Oracle Applications Adapter
Oracle Applications, integrating with PeopleSoft CRM, 29
Oracle Applications Adapter, configuring, 37-41
Oracle ERP, integrating with PeopleSoft CRM, 30

P

PeopleCode, 29
PeopleSoft CRM
  ATP checking, 28
  configuring, 42
  Oracle Applications, integrating with, 29
  Oracle ERP, integrating with, 30
  order status updates, 29
  sales order, creating, 28
PeopleSoft node
  configuring, 42-46
PubRatingPT port type, 134

Q

quote-to-order business process, 27

R

recieve activity, creating, 152
remote node, creating, 44
RIA. *See* Rich Internet Application
Rich Internet Application
  about, 76
  frontend, 77
rule
  creating, 67, 68
  editor, 68
  integrating into J2EE platform, 74
  layer, 65
rules engine, executing JRules, 72
ruleset
  exposing as web service, 70, 71
  invoking from BPEL, 72
  rules, creating, 67
runBuildScript() method, 56, 57

S

sales order, creating in PeopleSoft, 28
schemac utility, 118
scope, 19
scope activity, 19
security
  BPEL, 21
  business communication, 21, 22
  inbound, 22
  outbound, 21, 22
Service Support Environment, architecture, 52
solution architecture, BPEL process, 15
SSE, 52

W

Web Service Invocation Framework
  about, 115
  binding. *See* WSIF binding
web services
  exposing, 13-16
  layer, 65
  network, designing, 53-61
  orchestrating, 16, 18
Web Services Definition Language, 54
webMethods, expose as web service, 14
WSDL
  fault element, defining, 126
  session bean, 134
WSIF. *See* Web Service Invocation Framework
WSIF binding
  creating, using JDeveloper, 138-143
  defining, for Java exception, 126, 128
  EJB, using, 133-138
  Java class, defining, 120
  parts, 120

X

XML beans
  about, 132
  using, 132
XML facades, 116-118
XML serialization, 116
XQuery language
  about, 90
  generateActivity() method, 94

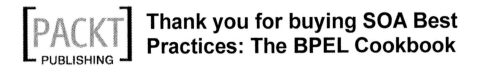

Thank you for buying SOA Best Practices: The BPEL Cookbook

About Packt Publishing

Packt, pronounced 'packed', published its first book "*Mastering phpMyAdmin for Effective MySQL Management*" in April 2004 and subsequently continued to specialize in publishing highly focused books on specific technologies and solutions.

Our books and publications share the experiences of your fellow IT professionals in adapting and customizing today's systems, applications, and frameworks. Our solution-based books give you the knowledge and power to customize the software and technologies you're using to get the job done. Packt books are more specific and less general than the IT books you have seen in the past. Our unique business model allows us to bring you more focused information, giving you more of what you need to know, and less of what you don't.

Packt is a modern, yet unique publishing company, which focuses on producing quality, cutting-edge books for communities of developers, administrators, and newbies alike. For more information, please visit our website: www.packtpub.com.

Writing for Packt

We welcome all inquiries from people who are interested in authoring. Book proposals should be sent to authors@packtpub.com. If your book idea is still at an early stage and you would like to discuss it first before writing a formal book proposal, contact us; one of our commissioning editors will get in touch with you.

We're not just looking for published authors; if you have strong technical skills but no writing experience, our experienced editors can help you develop a writing career, or simply get some additional reward for your expertise.

PUBLISHING

Business Process Execution Language
for Web Services
Second Edition

An architect and developer's guide to orchestrating web
services using BPEL4WS

Matjaz B. Juric   Benny Mathew   PACKT
Poornachandra Sarang

Business Process Execution Language for Web Services: Second Edition

ISBN: 1904811817   Paperback: 372 pages

An Architect's and Developer's Guide to BPEL and
BPEL4WS

1. Architecture, syntax, development, and
   composition of Business Processes and
   Services using BPEL

2. Advanced BPEL features such as
   compensation, concurrency, links,
   scopes, events, dynamic partner links,
   and correlations

3. Oracle BPEL Process Manager and BPEL
   Designer Microsoft BizTalk Server as a
   BPEL server

For more details:
http://www.packtpub.com/bpel2e/book

Please check **www.PacktPub.com** for information on our other titles

Printed in the United States
63528LVS00005B/137-162

9 781904 811336